Intercession: Prayer as Work

Revival in the Church

"And He saw that there was no man, and wondered that there was no intercessor."
Isaiah 59:16

"Wilt Thou not revive us again: that Thy people may rejoice in Thee?"
Psalm 85:6

J. Gordon Henry, Ed.D.

Printed in the USA
Printworks
701 Leesville Road
Lynchburg, Virginia 24502
434-239-5890

Other books by J. Gordon Henry
A Christian's Necessary Food
Adoration: Prayer as Worship
The Enabler
Hey! I'm Saved!
The Model Prayer
Notes from My Bible
Prayer Seminar Workbook
Spiritual Warfare
Upper Room Discourse

ISBN 1-882270-20-7

Dedication

To **Sue Troutman Henry**, who became
my wife on Thursday, April 18, 1957, and
who daily engages in ministry of
intercession for her family and the
prayer seminar ministry. A lasting image
of this woman of faith from many years
is in her private quarters with prayer notebook
in her hands praying for missions and
missionaries around the world.

and

To the 3 **M's** – **Mona Lee** (April 24,1958),
Mark Alan (October 8, 1959), and
Melody Ann (May 7, 1961) – our three children
who have brought joy and gladness to our hearts
since God gave them to us and who represent
an important part of our legacy to the world.

and

To the six grandchildren: William Edward Ware III
(Beau), Jeanne Leeann Ware Pribble, Wendy Henry Goodner,
James Alan Henry, Emilee Bradshaw Fulcher, and
Kimberlee Bradshaw.

and

The seven great-grandchildren: Caleb Roach,
Maggie Pribble, Willow Ware,
William Edward Ware IV (Stone), Lillian Goodner,
Emma Fulcher, and Elizabeth James Henry.

Preface

Prayer is the work that must come before all other work in the Lord's service. The sovereign God has ordained prayer as the tool to get His work done. God works only in concert with the praying of His people.

Few Christians are prayed for regularly by anyone after they become Christians. You can pretty well say to a new convert, "*I'm glad you came to Christ. I hope everything goes well for you. But you are on your own now.*"

In Isaiah's day, God looked down from Heaven and saw all the people living in Israel and Judah—and "*wondered that there were no intercessors*" (**Isaiah 59:16**).

Consider the people who live in the fifth house from your church building. Ask yourself if they have ever heard the name of Jesus in a saving sense one time. Are they going to Heaven when they die? Who is praying for them? The answer usually is "Nobody!" If you are not praying for your children, nobody else is. The need of the hour is intercessors!

Do you have the world on your heart, yet? Are you praying for those who are unreached with the Gospel? Are you praying for laborers? Are you praying for missionaries?

Most believers think that prayer is mostly prefix and suffix—what you do before you begin and finish work for the Lord. But prayer is the work that must undergird all other work—such as evangelism, teaching, or preaching.

Work implies spending energy. It is important to know that prayer itself requires energy and time. Prayer is work.

In order to become intercessors, it is important for a believer to understand biblical teachings that govern this aspect of praying. It is my hope that the studies that follow will not only provide basic knowledge, but will motivate you to become an intercessor by providing practical suggestions.

Yours in Calvary love,
J. Gordon Henry
Lynchburg, Virginia

Study One

"Then began men to call upon the name of the Lord."
Genesis 4:26b

As we move further into a new century, we have a wonderful opportunity to commit ourselves to service for the Lord Jesus Christ. There is abundant evidence in the Word of God that there is a land of beginning again for those who need it. We may be sure that God has told us what we need to know and that He does not ask us to do anything that we cannot—with His help—accomplish.

Dependence on God

One of the fascinating aspects of the prayer seminar ministry is the insight that comes to the teacher as he teaches the Word of God. In teaching **2 Chronicles 7:14,** it has become clear to me that being *"humble"* is the primary requisite for God to become active in our lives. The sense of *"humble"* is **dependence upon God and not upon our own strengths and resources.** God says that He will look to the person who is humble and who trembles at His Word **(Isaiah 66:2b)**. I'm relatively sure that He has provided the proper order for us to follow since a person is not likely to tremble at the Word who has an exalted opinion of himself that is manifested in pride. Before asking for God's hand to move (the meaning of "pray"), seeking His face, and turning from sin—the first requisite for God to move is humility—that is actually dependence on God—not self! Have you learned that lesson yet?

The very first of the characteristics of Kingdom citizens listed by the Lord Jesus Christ known as the Beatitudes **(Matthew 5:1-12)** deals with this spirit of dependence upon God since those who are poor in spirit are obviously not magnifying their own strengths. Pride would not be willing to acknowledge spiritual poverty. Jesus said, "Blessed are the poor in spirit" as the very beginning point for Kingdom citizens.

Prayer history began long ago

Since 1980, the author has conducted over six-hundred six-hour prayer seminars throughout the nation and the world. Soon he will have logged one million miles traveling to seminars. The basic teaching tool is the ***Prayer Seminar Workbook*** that is divided into nine sessions. The very first verse we use in Session One in the prayer seminar is **Genesis 4:26b**: *"Then began men to call upon the name of the Lord."* The context of this declaration is the birth of Seth's son who was given the name Enos, which means "weakness." With the coming of Enos, men became conscious of their weakness and need. Matthew Henry believed that the "then" was in the sense of seeing the effects of sin in Cain and Lamech that brought judgment. Thus, descendants of Seth wished to be distinguished as men who feared the Lord and who desired to do His will. Thus, prayer history began when need for God was acknowledged!

The greatest example of humility

We well know that the Lord Jesus Christ is the greatest example of humility. The *kenosis* (Gk.) passage in **Philippians 2:6-11** attests to His humility. The word *kenosis* means "to empty." Literally Jesus poured Himself out in order to do the will of the Father. He humbled Himself to become obedient to the death of the cross. The exalted Lord went to the cross as a servant—not to do His own will, but the will of God. A picture of His servanthood is seen in His washing the disciples' feet in the Upper Room during those last hours of His life on earth **(John 13)**. Although He was indeed both Master (Teacher) and Lord (one with authority to command), He laid aside His outer garment since the servant who usually greeted guests did not wear an outer robe, girded Himself with a towel, took a basin of water, fell on His knees since the disciples were reclining on a pallet on the floor, washed their feet, and wiped them dry with a towel.

We have the capacity to step outside ourselves and view ourselves rather objectively. I firmly believe that this is an ideal time to do that very thing. AM I DEPENDING ON THE LORD FOR HIS PROVISION OR AM I DEPENDING ON MY OWN ABILITIES AND RESOURCES? We have the capacity to make changes once we see what we need to do. Remember that God never asks us to do something that we cannot do with His help.

Humility is dependence and means that we look to God for everything we need. This sets us free from those things which can easily rob us of our joy: circumstances, people, and things. Genuine freedom comes when we arrive at the point that we need nothing but God. At that point nothing or no one can be a threat to us. We are free!

Prayer presupposes a sense of need

In my judgment, every element of prayer emanates from need. Prayer is bringing the need to worship, to be forgiven, to give thanks, to seek for ourselves and for others to God. As long as one is going to strut like the proverbial peacock, he will not have a prayer life.

During our seven-year ministry in the mountains of Kentucky, a favorite song which was often sung had the refrain, *"I don't know about tomorrow, but I know Who holds tomorrow and I know He holds my hand."* What better way to move through this final decade of the nineties than acknowledging this truth. Long ago, I learned **1 Peter 5:6-7**: *"Humble yourselves under the mighty hand of God, that He may exalt you in due time. Casting all your care upon Him, for He cares for you."* *"Humble"* means to acknowledge that God is working. There is a promise that if we will do this that He will exalt us in *"due time."* Most of us would like the exaltation to come today—or at least by tomorrow at this time. But it is up to God to set the parameters for the "due time" and it may be an extended period of time. Since God is good and merciful and remembers that we are dust **(Psalm 103:14)**, He has told us what to do during the interim while we wait for Him to exalt us: *"Casting all your care upon Him because He cares for you"* **(1 Peter 5:6-7)**.

As the leader of the prayer seminar ministry, I hereby acknowledge complete dependence upon God and submit the ministry to Him afresh and anew. What a joy it is to be entrusted with the task of calling God's children to Biblical praying. My prayer is that many believers will become prayer warriors.

Study Two

"You have not because you ask not . . . You ask and receive not because you ask amiss."

James 4:2b, 3a

In two brief, concise and clear declarations, James, through the inspiration of the Holy Spirit, has provided remarkably valuable insight into prayer. Due to the vital importance of understanding these two statements in gaining a proper perspective of prayer, there are two times in the prayer seminar that attention focuses on them. Repetition is the mother of learning.

Ask

In **II Chronicles 7:14**, we are told to humble ourselves, pray, seek God's face, and turn from sin. The result will be God's hearing from headquarters, forgiving our sin, and healing our land. Here, as other places in the Scripture, "pray" means "ask" in the sense of seeking God's hand to move either on behalf of self (petition) or others (intercession). Note that James does not say "pray" to explain his point; rather, he uses the word "ask" in the same sense of wanting **God's hand to move.** Clearly God has instructed His children to ask. Prayer is asking.

Motive

"**Amiss**" has to do with **wrong motive** in praying. "Why do I pray? Why do I ask?" This is the point being made. In the Sermon on the Mount, our Lord Jesus Christ dealt with the wrong motive in giving, praying, and fasting. In essence, He dealt with the public forms of worship zealously and assiduously practiced by the Scribes and Pharisees. Jesus explained that a desire for the attention and commendation of men for these acts was hypocrisy. A hypocrite is a person who does not want to *be* holy before God, but only to *appear* holy before men. Instead of being concerned about having the **reality** of righteousness, the Scribes and Pharisees only wanted the **reputation** of righteousness. The sense of "hypocrite" is the Greek actor's wearing a mask to portray someone he is not.

Paid in full

As He spoke of hypocritical giving, praying, and fasting, Jesus used a Greek word that cannot be adequately translated by one English equivalent. It is *apechoo,* made up of the preposition *apo*, meaning *"from"* and the verb *echoo,* meaning *"have"*. It is translated "reward" in the King James version. When this term is used, it indicates ***BEING PAID IN FULL WITH NO BALANCE LEFT OVER***. When rent was paid, this compound *apechoo* was used. The receipt was marked "**PAID IN FULL!**"

Jesus was teaching that if a person gives in order to be commended by onlookers, he is "paid in full" which means God will give him nothing in the world to come. However, if a person does not give to receive commendation from men, there is reward in the future. In regard to those who pray publicly to be commended, the same is true. They have their reward in full in this life. **Prayers meant for the ears of others never reach the ear of God.** The same is true in fasting.

It is possible to have the wrong motive in private, closet praying as well. A believer can even pray in the name of Jesus as he is instructed to do (Study **John 14:13,14; 15:6-8, 14, 16; 16:23-24, 26**—PRAY, but PRAY IN HIS NAME!) and still ask amiss which means that the motive is wrong. After all is said that can be said, **the bottom line related to proper motive is that God Himself will gain glory from whatever the answer to the prayer is**. The aim of prayer should never be any less or any lower than to bring glory to God. Is not this the meaning of the incredible promise Jesus made in **John 14:13** "*If you ask anything in my name that the Father will be glorified in the Son, I will do it*"?

Most of our prayers are for ourselves and our close kin. "Me and my wife—my son John, his wife, us four, no more." In most instances when we pray, we are motivated with selfishness, rather than the glory of God foremost in our hearts. By the way, this could be a place to start in getting on praying ground! If you have not already incorporated His glory into your praying, begin today. You will see quickly the difference that this makes!

Reminder: back to basics

During the series of intercession studies, I intend to provide the basics of praying. Many already have a handle on these truths, but there is a danger of neglecting what we know in times of blessing and prosperity. It has been the history of God's children to forget Him when things are going well. My first sermon in 1953, as a seventeen year-old preacher, dealt with this very issue. Israel was greatly blessed. They built "*goodly*

houses . . . their flocks multiplied . . . their gold increased"
(**Deuteronomy 8:12-13**). Then they forgot the Lord and
esteemed Him lightly, if at all. This has ever been the pattern.
By reminding us all of basics, we will have a time to do inventory to see where we are. My prayer is that these studies will
make a difference in the individual life of each reader and give
each an incentive to pass on to others what he learns.

Intercession: most important part

There needs to be a thorough understanding of the Biblical
teaching on intercession. In Exodus, I have been touched over
and over by the prayer life of Moses. "*And Moses returned unto
the Lord, and said, Oh, This people have sinned a great sin, and
have made them gods of gold, Yet now, if Thou wilt forgive their
sin; and if not, blot me I pray Thee out of Thy book which Thou
hast written*" (**Exodus 32:31-32**).

Among all the different phases or elements of prayer taught
in the Scriptures, intercession is the most important and
calculated to produce the most sublime blessings known to man.
Few Christians are prayed for regularly by anyone after they are
born into the family of God; even fewer unsaved people have
anyone calling their names personally before God. Within the
same household (living under the same roof) are believers who
do not pray regularly for each other and there are lost loved ones
living with believers and no one is praying regularly for the lost
loved ones. This ought not to be so! We need to understand and
practice the ministry of intercession. Do you understand who an
intercessor is and the importance that the Lord attaches to the
work of intercession?

Intercession defined

The word *intercession* comes from two Latin words that
mean *a go between*. An intercessor, therefore, is someone who
is standing between people or circumstances and God. That is
what Abraham did for Lot (**Genesis 18:22**). In intercession, we
are concerned for the needs and interests of others. Thus,
intercession is the unselfish aspect of prayer. The idea behind
the Greek word for intercession is "*to fall in with a person, to
draw near so as to converse freely, and hence to have freedom
of access.*" The word was used to describe a child's going to his
father on behalf of another, or a person's entering a king's
presence to submit a request. For you and me, **intercession is
prayer addressed to God the Father through the Lord Jesus**

Christ the Son in the power of the Holy Spirit for others. Intercession is acting as an intermediary between God and man.

Intercession illustrated

The prayer of our Lord, as recorded in **John 17**, is the greatest example of intercessory prayer. A few selections from this passage of God's Word will give us the very heart of this wonderful prayer and insight for our own prayers: *"I pray for them. I pray not for the world, but for them which You have given Me; for they are Yours. And all Mine are Yours, and Yours are Mine; and I am glorified in them. Holy Father, keep through Your own name those whom You have given Me, that they may be one, as We are. I pray not that You should take them out of the world, but that You should keep them from the evil [one]. Sanctify them through Your truth: Your Word is truth. Neither pray I for these alone, but for them also which believe on Me, that they may be with Me where I am; that they may behold My glory, which You have given Me; for You loved Me before the foundation of the world."* As our Lord faced death in just a few hours, He was not concerned about Himself in relation to the consequences that would follow His death upon the cross. Knowing the temptations, trials, and persecutions that awaited His followers, He poured out His heart in intercession to the Father for them. He prayed, also, for those who should believe on Him through their word. Further, His ministry of intercession continues forever in Heaven **(Hebrews 7:25, 9:24; Romans 8:34).** So, if we are to follow the **FOOTSTEPS OF JESUS**, we also must become intercessors.

The work needed is prayer

Prayer touches three worlds: heaven, earth, and hell. When it touches earth, it looks toward people and circumstances. That's **work!** The greatest of all needs in God's work today is prayer work. Without prayer work, all other work will have little permanent effect on anyone or anything. God's Word commands us to pray! Let's obey! It is wise to develop a written prayer list to use as you pray. Date each item. Pray Scriptures as much as possible. An example is to pray **Psalm 1:1-3** for a loved one. As you find similar passages, note them so that you will have them available as the Holy Spirit brings them to mind for specific people.

Plan for greatest impact

Spend time in each of the following studies until you understand the Biblical truths related to intercession. Be sure to review pages 8, 59-60 in the *Prayer Seminar Workbook.* Let's not become careless and lethargic about prayer and the Word! It is so easy to drift and neglect them for days on end. Plan for the greatest impact.

Study Three

"And He saw that there was no man, and wondered that there was no intercessor."

Isaiah 59:16

As I drove to the airport for a prayer seminar in Texas, a statement on a church marquee leaped out at me and vibrated my heart with rejoicing and excitement: **"The angel fetched Peter from the prison; prayer fetched the angel."** Isn't that right on target? In Study Two, background was provided on the work of **intercession** which is obviously **the most neglected element of prayer** in many lives. A simple definition was given for this element of prayer. Do you remember the definition? If not, you should go back and review. Don't forget that it is necessary to review and cause ourselves to remember previous learning. Some say that repetition is the mother of learning—and often it is so!

Standing between God and others

Intercession is from two Latin words meaning a **"go between."** Intercession is standing between God and someone else or some circumstance. The account of prayer fetching the angel to release Peter from prison is recorded in **Acts 12**. James, the brother of John, became the first martyr among the twelve disciples. Then Peter was arrested, imprisoned, and faced a similar fate at the hands of Herod the king. The **church met** at Mary's house (the mother of John Mark) and **prayed without ceasing** (v. 5). The intensity of their praying is reflected in the expression "without ceasing" which R. A. Torrey translates as "stretched-out-ed-ly" which pictures earnest and intense desire. SUCH PRAYING IS WORK. Prayer touches earth. When it does, it looks toward people and circumstances. That is WORK.

Intercession is the WORK that must be done if other Christian efforts such as evangelism and discipling are successful. When we are praying, we are doing the main WORK of ministry. **THE MAIN THING IS TO KEEP THE MAIN THING THE MAIN THING**. Since Satan knows that he cannot win the battle in the place of prayer, he makes every effort to keep the Christian from the place of prayer. Often his primary stratagem ("wile" **Ephesians 6:11**) is to keep us so

11

occupied doing good or neutral things that we have no time to get to the best thing—which is intercessory praying.

A major focus for the prayer seminar is to enlist prayer workers. My aim in teaching and sharing Scriptures for over five of the six hours in a seminar is to come to **"Seeking for others - Intercession"** on page 59 in the *Prayer Seminar Workbook*. During a prayer seminar, I always begin the final instruction on intercession by simply stating: *"The reason that I have come is to bring you to the point of becoming a prayer warrior. The biggest need in the church today is prayer WORK."* To WORK with the Holy Spirit in helping believers to understand prayer and to implant in their hearts and lives a hunger for the Divine that can not be satisfied outside the presence of God is the greatest joy in this ministry. As a fellow believer, you can share in this joy as a prayer warrior as well.

Been to work today

Have you been to WORK today in your place of prayer? Prayer is WORK. Prayer fetches the angel when the angel needs to be fetched. Prayer releases the supplies from the storehouse—whatever the item needed. There is always plenty in the storehouse. As you and I begin to pray, we can be sure God does not place us on back order. If you have not gone to WORK today, why not? Why do Christian neglect intercession?

Getting on praying ground

A major reason that many Christians do not engage in intercession is they are not on praying ground. During a prayer seminar, we do not cover Session Six in the workbook which is entitled "Getting Ready to Pray" and is sequel to session five, "The Sin of Prayerlessness." While the instruction provided in Session Five is designed to bring a believer face to face with sin in his life, to teach him how to be cleansed, and how to yield to the Holy Spirit, Session Six is designed for individual consideration. There is a checklist prepared by Jack Taylor which uses twenty-three Scriptures with key questions asked to allow the Holy Spirit to show us sin in our lives as a sample of how we can see ourselves as God sees us through the Word.

Getting on praying ground means that all known sins are confessed and forsaken. It further means that the believer has taken self off the control seat and yielded control to the Holy Spirit. We encourage each believer to look in the mirror of God's Word to see if you are on praying ground.

Unless you are on praying ground, you cannot pray for others. A priority should be to get on praying ground. You can use the material in the *Prayer Seminar Workbook* on pages 44-45 to have a personal confrontation with Holy God. It is obvious that the prayer that David prayed in **Psalm 139:23-24** must be our starting point. To be clean, we need to ask God to show us the sins in our hearts. If you need to do so, go back to page 37 in your *Prayer Seminar Workbook* and review the section on "How to be Spirit-filled," how to get on praying ground. Remember that "Spirit -filled" does not mean quantity since you received all the Holy Spirit that you are ever going to get the moment you received Christ as your Savior. Rather, "Spirit-filled" means "Spirit-controlled." Remember **Ephesians 5:18**? Just as a drunk man is controlled by the drink that is in him, so is the Spirit-filled man controlled by the Holy Spirit that is in him.

God uses clean vessels

God does not have to have gold or silver vessels; He does have to have a clean vessel. It is essential that we allow the Holy Spirit to show us sins in our lives and that we deal with each specific sin (not lumping them all together and saying "forgive me of all my sins, dear Lord" as we so often tend to do) that He brings to mind. If we don't do this, we simply will not get on praying ground and God will not hear and answer prayers **(Psalm 66:18, Isaiah 59:1-2)**.

Key words related to getting clean are **conviction**, **repentance**, and **confession**. Most believers do not know what these words mean. The Holy Spirit brings **conviction** which is **consciousness** of sin; it is our responsibility to respond to the conviction with repentance and confession. **Repentance is changing our minds** about the sin; **confession is naming the sin specifically,** agreeing with God that it is in our lives and is wrong (looking at it from God's point of view saying the same thing about it that God has said), and receiving **forgiveness and cleansing (1 John 1:9).**

You will likely be surprised at some of the sins that the Holy Spirit will bring to your mind when you ask God to show you your sins. A list that I recently confronted was arrogance, conceit, selfishness, rebellion, impure thoughts, human wisdom. After you have requested a "full-scale investigation" and have dealt with sins that are revealed in your life, don't forget to ask: "Is there anything else?" Don't be surprised when another one comes on the screen! It is often at this point that the little things come forward that we ordinarily would not think about—but which obviously offend God. The closer a believer gets to God, the more conscious he will be of his sins. Remember Isaiah 6?

Then the Holy Spirit will help

Only when a person is on praying ground can he become a prayer warrior and begin the **WORK** of intercession. Once he is clean, the Holy Spirit will help in praying; otherwise, he will not pray with power. **Romans 8:26** is one of the most encouraging verses in the Word of God for the intercessor. *"Likewise the Spirit also helps in our weaknesses. For we do not know what we should pray for as we ought, but the Spirit Himself makes intercession for us with groanings which cannot be uttered."* We have a weakness that we cannot overcome alone; simply, we do not know what to pray for as we should. The Holy Spirit joins us to make up the difference. He knows how to bring our request before God. The Holy Spirit will not join until a believer is clean and has surrendered control to the Holy Spirit.

The Word of God will help

You can expect the Holy Spirit to draw you to the written Word of God. God speaks to us in His Book, the Bible. We learn to pray according to God's will in the Book in which His will is revealed. We **hear, read, study,** and **memorize** the Word so that we can **meditate** on the Word. Once the Word of God is in our minds, the Holy Spirit can take it and bring it alive as we begin to pray. Prayer becomes God-centered, rather than self-centered. The only way to renew our minds (**Romans 12:2**) is through the Word of God. Study carefully each Bible study related to prayer and the Word with anticipation. God is ready when we are! As you grow in your prayer life, you will actually begin to pray the Word of God for yourself and others!

Ready to go to work

Intercession is the part of prayer that brings the greatest results and dividends. It is the most neglected part of prayer because we are not on praying ground. Once we are clean, we can go to WORK. We will then "stir ourselves" (**Isaiah 64:7**) to lay hold on God. There will be movement, effort and discipline—there will be WORK. It is absolutely necessary for us to WORK if we are going to make progress toward being a prayer warrior. There are some things that God does not do for us; rather, He waits until we do them. We put food, water, and oxygen into our bodies. There follows a process of manufacturing energy from these ingredients. We then expend that energy. Most of the energy is spent on activities that really don't matter at all yet they take our time and resources. Twenty-four hours after we do them, it doesn't matter if we did them at all. If we are going to **use our energy on things that do matter,** it will be because we have made up our minds to do so. THE MAIN THING IS TO KEEP THE MAIN THING THE MAIN THING! **The less we pray for ourselves and the more we pray for others, the nearer we approach Christlikeness.**

Study Four

"And He saw that there was no man, and wondered that there was no intercessor."

Isaiah 59:16

On the basis of a belief that each Christian should continue to develop his own prayer life and become an intercessor, this is the fourth study featuring basics in intercessory prayer. It is necessary for us to review the Biblical principles in order to keep the proper perspective on prayer. A good way to get your brain in gear is to ask yourself to recall what the Holy Spirit has taught you. What is it you have now learned about prayer? Think about it. As Jack Taylor has said, *"No believer's practice of prayer will rise to stay above his view of prayer—thus the need to constantly keep a proper perspective on prayer."* (**Prayer Seminar Workbook**, page 10). We continue the series on intercession.

An intercessor is one who stands between God and people/circumstances/nations. The picture is God in Heaven and people on earth with a believer interceding—serving as a go-between. All of us need the support of intercessors; in addition, every believer needs to be an intercessor. This is the work that must be done in order for the other efforts to serve the Lord to make any difference.

Intercessors needed

AT THIS MOMENT ON THIS VERY DAY ARE YOU STANDING BETWEEN GOD AND SOMEONE ELSE? Could it be that God WONDERS where the intercessors are for the 284 million people in the United States? Through intercessory prayer, power will be focused on individuals in a way that will break down barriers. Recently, I heard of an incident in a church that well illustrates the relationship of prayer and power. As the organist began to play to begin a Sunday morning service, no sound of music came forth from the instrument. The time necessary for the repair was estimated and a note was sent to the pastor that read: "The power will be on after your morning prayer." Prayer indeed makes the difference between operating in man's power or God's power.

Praying for fellow believers

17

The primary motivation in beginning a prayer chapel ministry in Virginia with around-the-clock praying was to provide intercessory prayer support for fellow believers. Sad to say, few Christians are prayed for regularly by anyone and that should not be so. Every local church needs to develop a prayer strategy whereby believers pray for one another by name and need. Paul illustrates this type of intercession when he told the Roman believers: *"I thank my God through Jesus Christ for you all"* **(Romans 1:8).** Prayer (1) to God the Father, (2) through the Lord Jesus Christ the Son (3) for others—that is intercessory praying—and (4) in the power of the Holy Spirit Who joins us as we begin to pray.

A study of Paul's praying provides the primary direction for his praying—which is quite foreign to what we pray for others. In **Ephesians 3:14-19**, he prays not for physical or material blessings, but for spiritual blessings. He prays that there may be **spiritual strength (v. 16), spiritual depth (v. 17), spiritual perspective (v. 18),** and **spiritual fullness (v. 19).** Think what a difference possessing these characteristics would make in a believer's life and in the cause of the Lord Jesus Christ.

So very often we hear about failure in individual Christian lives and in the church fellowship that can be traced back to failures in daily prayer and reading the Word. Sometimes, a prominent Christian leader loses his influence and brings dishonor to the name of the Lord Jesus Christ. Where are the prayer warriors who are placing a hedge of protection around fellow Christians? When we do pray for others, it is often crisis-oriented praying instead of ongoing steady praying. Think about your prayer life for fellow believers. Start with your immediate family and work beyond that. **You can be sure if you are not praying for your spouse, your children, or your grandchildren no one else is.** As an intercessor, pray the Scripture truths that the Holy Spirit gives you in relationship to other believers.

Praying for our nation

Are you as dismayed and shocked as I am about the organized effort to get rid of God in the United States to make us a completely secular, humanistic society? Committees of Correspondence are being organized across America to generate letters and opposition to all things Christian in education, in government, and in society in general. When the first negative Supreme Court rulings came during the Warren Court in the

50's, Billy Graham noted that when a nation sows to the wind, it will reap a whirlwind. As we look at the wars (crime, drugs, immorality, pornography) being waged against America's moral values that have guided us historically, it is obvious that we are simply reaping what we have been sowing. **As our moral code has disintegrated more and more with each passing year, there have been catastrophic results.**

National Day of Prayer

Since 1952, there has been a day set aside each year as a National Day of Prayer. It seems very appropriate to devote the remainder of study four on praying for our nation—with its 284 million people—to this day. Many across America have caught on to the value of such a day in our history and we want others to do the same. There should be some kind of organized praying in every church building for our nation on the first Thursday in May. Though days of prayer are found throughout our history and the National Day of Prayer has been observed since 1952, it has only had a specific calendar date authorized by Congress since 1988. The National Day of Prayer has great significance for us as a nation. It has been the foundation on which our country was established. The early Pilgrims engaged diligently in prayer. Today both houses of Congress open their sessions daily with prayer.

Certainly we need to come together to repent and confess sins and to ask for God's mercy. That is what Daniel did (see **Daniel 9**). God is the only one able to change the appetites, the hearts, and the minds of men. We need to ask Him to intervene in America as never before. We need to pray for leaders to come on the scene who will follow God's way in preserving a strong, moral nation.

Many times such days of special occasion are neglected. Our attention is diverted elsewhere to many good things— programs, schedules, activities—which invade our lives nullifying our participation in national repentance and confession. We are reminded that we have not, because we ask not (**James 4:2b**). There is no doubt that only God can spare America from self-destruction. Nothing can surpass the necessity, the failure and the results of genuine deep prayer by His children. After all, the formula given in **2 Chronicles 7:14** for the healing of a nation includes prayer.

Following is a prayer guide compiled by Norval Hadley of World Vision, member of the National Prayer Committee, to be used on the National Day of Prayer. It can be used for any other day of the year as well. Since 1988, the J. Gordon Henry Ministries has served as the Tennessee coordinator for the National Day of Prayer. Since our seminars have been conducted in 40 states, it is possible to encourage pockets of prayer for our nation in a wide area. I encourage you to determine to participate personally in the National Day of Prayer. Include your family. Further, I encourage you to be responsible for bringing before the people in your local community and in your local church the need for a day of prayer for America. If you need additional ideas or guidance, contact us. We will appreciate having a report on what you did and the results after the National Day of Prayer.

Prayer guide for National Day of Prayer
7:00 a.m. Proverbs 14:34. At 6:00 a.m. on the National Day of Prayer, hundreds of people are gathered at several sites in our nation's capitol for a sunrise prayer meeting, and now as you are praingy there is an all-day prayer meeting in Washington's Senate Office Building. Each half hour, prayer will be directed by a difference national leader, all this under sponsorship of the National Prayer Committee. Pray that God will hear the prayers of earnest Christians, today, all across our nation and that this National Day of Prayer will mightily bless our land.

7:30 a.m. Psalm 147. Let this be a half hour of worship and praise with humble gratitude to God for what He has done for us, for the way He has blessed our nation, guided its leaders, strengthened our churches, protected us from enemies, and preserved our freedoms.

8:00 a.m. Psalm 66:18, Isaiah 59:1-2. Use this half hour for the prayer of confession. First, be sure you have no unconfessed sin in your own life, for God will not hear when there is unconfessed and unforsaken sin. Then pray with the attitude of the Apostle Paul in **Romans 9** in confession and repentance for the sins of our nation.

8:30 a.m. Proverbs 28:2. Pray for our President. Ask God to give him great wisdom as he provides the leadership for our nation. Ask that he will have the ability to discern right from wrong, truth from fiction, God's will from man's will. Pray against forces that are operating to weaken the presidency.

9:00 a.m. I Timothy 2:1-4. Pray for our nation's leaders who surround the president. Pray by name for Vice President Al Gore. Pray for cabinet officers and staff, military leaders and ambassadors. Pray for the members of the Supreme Court: William Rehnquist, Byron R. White, Harry A. Blackmun, John

Paul Stevens, Sandra Day O'Connor, Antonin Scalia, Anthony M. Kennedy, David H.Souter, Clarence Thomas, William F. Burger, Lewis F. Powell, Jr., and Ruth Bader Ginsberg. Pray that there will be purity in their thoughts and deeds, that God will protect them from the corrosive effect of the power they handle. Stable leadership must be in place to allow us to lead "*quiet and peaceable*" lives (**1 Timothy 2:2**).

9:30 a.m. Ephesians 6:10-18; 2 Thessalonians 2:9. Pray for members of the Congress, especially your senators and representative. Ask that God will give these legislative leaders discernment to make good decisions against the powers of evil, that they will be given wisdom to lead so God's kingdom can come and His "will be done on earth (in our country) as it is in Heaven."

10:00 a.m. Psalm 127:1, Romans 12:1-5. Pray for your governor, lieutenant governor, state senators, state representatives, county commissioners, the mayor and city officials, judges and court officials, public and private school authorities, and law enforcement officials. Use the same requests suggested in the two items above.

10:30 a.m. John 17:11, Acts 4:29, I Timothy 4:4. Pray for our churches and church-related organizations; for pastors, evangelists, chaplains, teachers, deacons, elders, lay people, missionaries, Bible and Theological schools and all outreach ministries. Pray especially for the ones close to you. Ask that personal renewal will result in spiritual and moral awakening in our nation (**2 Chronicles 7:14**).

11:00 a.m. 2 Corinthians 5:17-20. Psalm 85:6, Matthew 28:19-20. Pray for the ministry of reaching the lost with the gospel message, that Christians will be vital witnesses for Christ through their lives and words, resulting in many turning to Christ and reformation in our society. Pray for spiritual strength and integrity in our nation's churches and pray for the pastors.

11:30 a.m. Psalm 113:5-7. Pray for the homeless. There are reported to be about 3 million now in our country, and the number is growing by 20% a year. Thirty percent of them are chronically mentally ill, and 500,000 of them are children. Many of them are coming to the church, because they have nowhere else to turn, and the church still has no visible program to help. Pray for the ministries of rescue missions and that church and government will find better ways to solve the problems of the homeless.

12 noon. Luke 4:16-21. You are now praying with thousands who "take 5 at 12" spending at least five minutes in prayer at noon on this day. Pray for the poor and for agencies that minister to their needs. Pray that our churches will learn how to do a better job of addressing the root causes of poverty, and that church and government programs to help them will not destroy incentive or human dignity. There was an increase of 38% living under the poverty level between 1978 and now. Eighty percent of the children born in our ghettos are born out of wedlock. The largest poverty group is in homes headed by single women.

12:30 p.m. Hebrews 13:3, John 8:36, Psalm 91:14-16. Pray for those who are prisoners and for ministries to them, like Prison Fellowship, M-2, Good News Mission, and others. In 1994, there were over around one million in federal and local prisons, and the number is growing ten times as fast as the general population. Include those who are prisoners to drugs, alcohol, immorality, obscenity, pornography, crime, prejudice, hunger, illness, unbelief, and despair. Remember their families. Ninety percent lost their marriages while in prison.

1:00 p.m. Colossians 2:8, Proverbs 1:7. Pray for greater Christian impact on mass media. Pray for the TV, radio, and film industries. A recent study showed that nearly all sex on TV soap operas is between unmarried people. When a Christian leader is depicted in a TV drama, he is usually the subject of ridicule. Pray against pornography in films and magazines. Pray specifically for your local newspaper. Pray for commentators to be fair.

1:30 p.m. Deuteronomy 5:16, Ephesians 5:22-6:4. Pray for American homes. Pray for men and women as they contemplate marriage, for couples who are experiencing stress in their marriages, for parents who need wisdom and courage to nurture their children in godly traditions, for children to respect their parents and other authority. There are 2.5 million runaway kids, plus another 2.5 million throwaway kids. There are 6,000 teenagers who commit suicide each year plus another 500,000 who try. Pray for a restoration of the American family. Pray for the power of God to come against physical and mental abuse of wives and children in our homes.

2:00 p.m. Jeremiah 32:27, Psalm 60:12. Pray that America's spiritual shackles will be broken so ungodly practices like abortion on demand can be corrected. One Congressman reported that there are five lobbying groups working in Washington on this issue, but they were so divided on minor issues they cannot make meaningful progress. He felt prayer is the only thing that will break the deadlock.

2:30 p.m. Jeremiah 31:9, 15-17. Pray for deliverance from the terrible blight of drug abuse. At least 24 million in our country are known to have used cocaine; ten percent in our high school are users. First graders have been found behind schools smoking pot. Because of competition, the potency of marijuana now is up to sixteen times what it was at first. To show the power of this blight, heroin can be bought in Taiwan at $7-$11 a kilo, and when cut it can be sold in Los Angeles for $2 million. Wars are waged in our streets to gain control of this kind of money. The efforts of law enforcement alone have proven inadequate in dealing with the problem. Christians must pray down the power of God.

3:00 p.m. Psalm 119:126, Isaiah 49:25. Pray for our nation's private and public schools and universities. Pray for Christian teachers in public schools, and for Christian influence on school boards and PTAs. Ask God to replace professors who mislead our young by teaching that there are no moral absolutes, that all moral standards are flexible and relative. Pray that deceitful and harmful literature in our schools will be exposed and expelled.

3:30 p.m. Isaiah 32:17-18. Pray for health services, community services, cultural programs and scientific research. Pray for the people and the agencies that provide these services. Ask God to give us the solution to the "welfare mentality" that is prevalent in all states. Pray that graft and waste will be exposed and eliminated.

4:00 p.m. Proverbs 3:7-10. Pray for our nation's economy, for businesses, and businessmen. Pray we will have the will to turn from deficit spending, that God will come against all that saps our economic strength. Thank God for the wealth we enjoy, and pray that we will be good stewards of it.

4:30 p.m. Numbers 16:44-50. Pray with humility and repentance over the disease AIDS. The surgeon general has reported that it has reached pandemic proportions. There are probably more infected than any of us know. Pray that we will respond to this tragedy with a return to monogamy and fidelity. Pray especially for innocent victims.

5:00 p.m. Ecclesiastes 11:9-10, Acts 2:16-19. Pray for our nation's young people. Ask God to protect them, give them strength to say "no" to sin, and give them the will to prepare well for service and leadership. Pray that sons and daughters shall prophesy and young men shall see visions.

5:30 p.m. Isaiah 31:1. Pray over our nation's relationships with other nations, that leaders and ambassadors who have responsibility for foreign policy will have God's wisdom and strength. Pray for those that participate in arms talks, that America will be a strong force for peace and justice in the world.

6:00 p.m. Hosea 6:10, Mark 4:22. Historian Richard Lovelace said that the late eighties were the worst in the history of evangelical Christianity public relations-wise. Use this half hour to pray with vicarious repentance over the process by which God is purging His Church to prepare it for powerful ministry in spiritual awakening. Pray for fallen evangelists and their families, and that other spiritual leaders will repent and turn from sin to avoid further wounding the body of Christ.

6:30 p.m. 2 Chronicles 7:14. People all across America have humbled themselves and prayed today. Some have turned from wicked ways. Now believe God to fulfill His promise, to hear our prayers, forgive our sins, and heal our land. Praise Him for what He is going to do.

Study Five

"I have set watchmen on your walls, O Jerusalem, Who shall never hold their peace day or night. You who make mention of the Lord do not keep silent, and give Him no rest till He establishes and till He makes Jerusalem a praise in the earth."
Isaiah 62:6-7

On the basis of a belief that believers should become active prayer warriors, this is the fifth study featuring basics in intercessory prayer. You might ask yourself what you remember from the previous four studies. Review assists learning. As previously stated, in a sense repetition is the mother of learning. While rote memory does not necessarily bring about understanding and insight, it is important to get truths implanted into the mind—knowing that the Holy Spirit cannot use what is not there to assist us in our understanding. If you find that you cannot remember key ideas already shared, now is a good time for the review. By this time you should understand the basic meaning of intercession. You should have insight into prayer as work. There should be a clear perception of the role of the Lord Jesus Christ in intercession. You should know, also, that a requisite of intercession is being clean before the Lord—otherwise your prayers will not be heard (**Psalm 66:18; Isaiah 59:1-2**).

During this study, I will deal with some thoughts about praying for individuals with primary emphasis on fellow believers. Other subjects that will be covered in the remaining studies are as follows: praying for the lost, praying for our nation, and praying for world evangelization including how to pray for missionaries and how to pray for pastors.

Background

There are three background areas that need a word. First, prayer takes time. During the past few days, I have been impressed with the **necessity of investing the needed time** to pray effectively. Somehow it is imperative that we understand that we will never be effective prayer warriors when we spend ten minutes in prayer and three hours watching a baseball game on the television. Unless there is willingness to set aside quality time for intercession, we will most likely make little difference as a prayer warrior. While it is true that everyone has as much time as anyone else, one of the subtle tactics of Satan is to assure us that we are too busy to spend much time in prayer. The amount of time we allow for prayer is an index of the real importance we attach to it. Some of us have become so engrossed on majoring on the minors that there is little time left for really important matters.

The second area is having the required **burden** to pray. Without a definite burden, there is little incentive to exercise the discipline needed to pray. Note in **Psalm 126:5-6** that we are told that results come when there is a burdened heart. Unless the gospel seed is watered with tears of concern, there will be little impact even if we go forth bearing the precious seed (which is the Word of God). A clear view of eternity is necessary for a burden. This will come only from knowing the Word of God. As a seventeen-year-old pastor in 1953, I remember vividly the burdens that developed as the Holy Spirit took the Word and made it live in minds. It seems to me that television and prosperity came along to rob believers of their burdens—which has made a tremendous negative impact on spirituality.

The third area is using the authority that we have in Christ to ask God specifically to bind the power of Satan (**Matthew 18:18; Mark 3:27).** We are called of God to be conquerors in spiritual warfare on this earth (**Ephesians 6:11,12).** James describes this warfare when he told us to submit ourselves to God and to resist the Devil so he will flee from us (**James 4:7).** This should not make us afraid; in fact, it should give us great encouragement in our role as intercessors. We have power in this warfare; the Lord Jesus Christ Himself is that power (**Ephesians 6:10).** We must stand our ground in this spiritual battle with the authority given us by God. Strongholds cannot stand against our authority when it is properly wielded (**2 Corinthians 10:4-5).** Just as a policeman can stop or move traffic by a gesture of his hand, so we, in Christ's name, command spiritual powers. Through prayer (in His name—by His authority—based on His shed blood) believers can command evil powers that bind the souls of people to release their captives. We will explore this more fully in the next study when we deal with praying for the lost. Remember that Satan is perfectly defeated and greater is He who is in us than the one that is in the world (**1 John 4:4).**

Praying for others

Intercession is praying for others. In intercession, we are concerned for the needs and interests of others. The idea behind the Greek word is "to fall in with a person, to draw near so as to converse freely, and hence to have freedom of access." It is the word used to describe a child who goes to his father on behalf of another, or a person who enters a king's presence to submit a petition. There is a responsibility that must be accepted to intercede for others. The intercessor is acting as an intermediary between God and man. He forgets himself and his own needs in his identification with the needs of the one for whom he prays.

The prayers of Abraham for the people of Sodom (**Genesis 18:23-33**) and of Moses for Israel (**Exodus 32:1-14**) are classic examples of intercession. How do we move beyond a superficial, surface request for God to "bless" a person? A starting point is to believe that we have a living God who exercises direct influence on the affairs of men. Then we need to take hold of the living God just as Jacob did, and tell Him, "*I will not let you go unless you bless me with a prayer ministry that will help others in the battle and bring glory to you*" (**Genesis 32:26**). Then we need to move to spiritual or eternal matters and not be bogged down with the material or trivial—which is so easy to do.

Suppose that you have a loved one who is going through a difficult circumstance such as being thrown into the lion's den or going through the water or fire. As a rule, the thrust of our praying is for deliverance. Daniel was not kept **out** of the lion's den; he was kept **in** the lion's den. If we understand that we need to pray for spiritual lessons to be learned, we can pray that God will be glorified in the time of stress by the actions and reactions of our loved one. We can ask that he will receive God's more-than-ample provision as he learns the lessons God has in this trial.

Listen to the Holy Spirit

Be sensitive to what the Holy Spirit leads you to pray. Often, He will bring to your mind a specific Scripture that will serve as the request you make during your time of intercession. Pray fervently to be led by the Holy Spirit to the exact needs of the one in Christ for whom you pray. There will be times when you will sense a need to pray for some person. Obey. Note the hour, day and date. Then be alert to the results of your prayer.

How to pray for others

There is a difference between simply praying for people and genuine intercession. During the past few years, I have had occasional correspondence with Rev. Will Bruce, Overseas Missionary Fellowship, who has developed a strong interest in prayer. Some of his insights are worth passing along. While he alerts his readers that his insights are not exhaustive, he suggests seventeen points to guide us in our intercession that are worth our careful consideration.

Pray that the person for whom we are interceding will:

1. Realize his present exalted position in Christ. Many believers are ignorant that through the work of the Lord Jesus Christ on the cross, we have an exalted position before God. It is only as we acknowledge who we really are in Christ that we can live that new identity that is ours.

2. Present himself as a living sacrifice. The ultimate and totally necessary step of Christian dedication is presenting our bodies and all we have and are as a living sacrifice to God. While this commitment is not essential to salvation, no progress will be made in the Christian life without it.

3. Be filled with the Holy Spirit. Being controlled by the Holy Spirit is not optional equipment for the Christian. Nothing in the spiritual life can be accomplished without His power. Pray that the believer will allow the Holy Spirit to work daily in his life.

4. Be regular and systematic in the study of God's Word. Satan persists in cutting Christians off from the Source—being daily in the Word and prayer. His efforts have caused many believers to conclude that the things of the world are not so bad and the things of God are not so important.

5. Have the mind of Christ. Pray that the believer will have the mind of Christ in regard to priorities, goals, and guidance, with sharpened insights so as not to waste time on good things and miss God's best. Pray that he will constantly live with eternity's values in view.

6. Grow daily in Christlike maturity. Pray that the believer will see clearly the need to grow in grace toward maturity.

7. Appropriate the full armor of God. There is full protection provided. Pray that the believer will have his eyes opened to the dangers of Satanic attacks and will put on the full armor of God.

8. Be alert to Satan's strategy. Pray that the believer will not only be kept from sin, but also will be aware of the threefold

Satanic temptations: the lust of the flesh, the lust of the eyes, and the pride of life **(1 John 2:16)**. Pray that he will know that victory comes only as he takes the victory of Calvary as his own **(I Corinthians 15:57-58)**. Pray that he will discern between Satanic pressure and godly chastening.

9. Not love the world system. Pressures from peers, the media, and the world increasingly oppose Biblical standards. Pray that he will love God and not the world **(I John 2:15-17)**.

10. Have a spirit of brokenness and humility. God promises to look toward the person who is humble and trembles at His Word **(Isaiah 66:2b)**. Humility is an attitude of dependence upon God and not self.

11. Have a servant's heart. Pray that the believer will desire to serve God and others—which is the essence of Christianity.

12. Build a Scriptural family. Pray that the one for whom you are praying will look neither to the world nor to carnal Christians, but to the Word of God for understanding of family responsibilities. Pray that husband and wife will maintain a balance among family, ministry, and job responsibilities. Pray that parents will be firm and loving—ever realizing the importance of being godly models for their children. Pray for those who are single to look to the Lord for the choice of a life partner.

13. Become an effective prayer warrior. Pray that the believer will understand what it means to be a prayer warrior; few do. Pray that his praying will be Biblically based, specific, consistent, steadfast in the Spirit, in faith, and with understanding.

14. Know God's hand on him in physical and material things. Pray that the one you are praying for will have a measure of health that will best glorify God. Pray that, when set aside by ill health, he will learn the lessons God has for him and draw upon Divine resources. Pray also for safety in travel, financial provision in keeping with God's plan for him, and proper use of the time and money God entrusts to him.

15. Learn to praise the Lord. Praise brings glory to God. Pray that the person for whom you are praying will enter a praise life—centered in the praise and adoration of the Triune God that will result in joy, power, adoration, and glory to the Lord. Pray that he will give thanks for his potential in Christ, for his spiritual growth, and for the resources available in Christ.

16. Engage in a life of prayerful worship. True worship is true service. Pray that the believer will not be on a works treadmill substituting activity for true worship and time with the Lord. Pray that he will make **Psalm 37:3-7** the basis of his spiritual life. "***Trust** in the Lord. . . **delight** yourself in the Lord. . . **commit** your way to the Lord. . . **be still** before the Lord . . . **wait** patiently for Him . . . and He will give you the desires of your heart.*"

17. Reach out to the unsaved. Pray that the one for whom you are praying will love the lost as the Lord Jesus does and will reach out to a lost and dying world with the message of salvation.

Some should be intercessors

Do you see some implications for your own intercession through Rev. Bruce's suggestions? Prayer is God's method for getting His work done. We need to hold other people up before God. We will never have genuine revival unless we learn to pray. Intercession is the greatest ministry in the Body of Christ, yet it is the most neglected in the church today. In Isaiah's day, God *"wondered that there were no intercessors"* for Israel **(Isaiah 59:16)**.

There are some of you who should consider the ministry of intercession as God's calling for your lives. God needs a person to *"stand in the gap and make up the hedge"* **(Jeremiah 5:1; Ezekiel 22:30)**. Could it be that His call is expressly for you to become a prayer warrior? Interceding for others is the most Christlike, unselfish praying that you and I will ever do! When a Christian becomes an intercessor—one who stands in the gap between a gracious God and a needy people—he is then in a very true and real sense Christ-like because preeminently Christ is our Mediator, our Advocate, our High Priest, our Go-between **(I Tim. 2:5; I John 2:1, 2; Hebrews 3:1; 7:25; 9:24)**. The greatest ability is availability! *"Pray one for another . . . the effectual fervent prayer of a righteous man availeth much"* **(James 5:16)**.

Speaking of what God has revealed and done during our intercession can easily lead to pride. God knows the weakness of the human heart toward this sin and has warned us. Unless He definitely prompts us to share, we should remain silent. *"And they kept silent and told no one in those days anything they had seen"* **(Luke 9:36)**.

Study Six

"And I sought for a man among them, that should make up the hedge, and stand in the gap before me for the land, that I should not destroy it: but I found none. Therefore have I poured out mine indignation upon them; I have consumed them with the fire of my wrath; their own way have I recompensed upon their heads, saith the Lord God."

Ezekiel 22:30-31

There are many facets of intercession which we have now covered. In this study, the theme is praying for the lost. Although the whole idea of intercession is a mystery that can never be answered completely, it is God's will that He operates in answer to prayer. Prayer enables God to do things He would otherwise not do. Prayer is not a means to get man's will done in Heaven; rather, prayer is God's ordained means for getting God's will done on earth.

A vivid example of the importance of intercession is found in the text above when judgment fell on a nation after God's failure to find a person to stand in the gap for the land. God needed a man to stand in the gap for the land that He would not destroy it. The practice of intercession can keep the wrath of God from coming upon an individual or a nation. Do you understand this truth? Do you believe this truth? Another example is the time the intercession of Moses prevailed when God was going to destroy the people **(Exodus 32:11-14)**.

Background

Paul expressed his burden to pray for his people, Israel, that *"they might be saved"* **(Romans 10:1)**. He described his burden as *"great heaviness and continual sorrow in (his) heart"* **(Romans 9:2)**. The context **(9:1-3)** includes a statement that the Holy Spirit is his witness that he is telling the truth—since the treatment he had received from his own people would lead an observer to question his veracity in the matter. He sounded much like Moses interceding for Israel **(Exodus 32:11-14)** when he shared that his burden was so intense that he would be willing to go to hell if his people could be saved. As noted last month, there is little incentive to exercise the discipline needed to pray without a burdened heart. Results are assured when there is a burdened heart **(Psalm 126:5-6)**. As the gospel seed is watered

31

with tears of concern, the precious seed (which is the Word of God) will have great impact. Since we are so preoccupied with this life, it is so easy simply to forget life in eternity—which will either be Heaven or Hell—based on what a person does with the Lord Jesus Christ.

Praying for the lost

We can be confident that when we ask anything according to His will, God hears us and will answer (**1 John 5:14-15**) our requests. What is His will concerning the salvation of the unsaved? God is "*long-suffering to us-ward, not willing that any should perish, but all should come to repentance.*" (**2 Peter 3:9**). "All" includes everyone in this incontrovertible statement of God's desire. He wants "all" to come to repentance. He loves the whole world (**John 3:16**). Christ is the propitiation for the sins of "*the whole world*" (**1 John 2:2**).

Paul's charge to Timothy is that he pray "*for all men*" and that "*God our Savior [would] have all men to be saved, and to come unto the knowledge of the truth*" and that "*Christ Jesus. . . gave Himself a ransom for all*" (**1 Timothy 2:1, 3-6**). Therefore, **praying for the lost is a very important need in intercession.** Our intercession frees God to do some things He would not otherwise do; God has chosen to involve us in His plan and has chosen to limit Himself to our praying. What an awesome thought! With confidence we can pray for the lost because saving the lost is His will.

As we recount how to pray for the lost, it is important to be specific—not general. Intercede for a particular lost person BY NAME—not just all lost people. Name the person in prayer and focus your thoughts and prayers toward that person. This is an extremely important part of praying for the lost. Remember that few people ever come to Christ until someone begins to pray for them as individuals.

Three directions for praying for the lost

There are three directions to focus your praying for the lost: toward Satan, toward the Savior, and toward the Saints.

Toward Satan. The first target should be Satan. It is the power of Satan that holds the sinner in bondage. You will remember that Jesus did not deal with surface problems, but the power behind the problems. When Jesus revealed to the disciples that He would go to Jerusalem, where He would suffer many things, be killed, and raised again the third day, Simon Peter told Him that He did not know what He was talking about.

Jesus realized the power behind Peter's remark and targeted Satan: *"Get thee behind Me, Satan"* was his response (**Matthew 16:21-23**).

Paul spoke directly to the demon who possessed the young girl in Philippi (**Acts 16:16-18**). He further described spiritual warfare pointing out that we are not to use carnal weapons in the flesh, but spiritual weapons that can pull down the strongholds that enslave people (**2 Corinthians 10:3-5**). By the way, note that the strongholds are in the mind—"imaginations", "knowledge" and "thought." In **Ephesians 6:12,** Satan's spiritual hierarchy of organization is given. Satan is not omnipotent, omniscient, or omnipresent, but he is organized. After a believer gets his armor on, the first activity mentioned is prayer (v. 18) since prayer is where the battle is fought.

The primary focus of evangelism is toward Satan. A lost person is "bound by the god of this world" and is in the *"snare of the devil taken captive by him at his will"* (**2 Timothy 2: 25-26**). He has *"blinded the minds of them which believe not"* (**2 Corinthians 4:4**). The devil is the *"strong man"* who must first be bound (**Matthew 12:29**) and Jesus is the One who is stronger than the devil who can bind him (**Luke 11:21-22**). Through prayer, we need to appropriate the truth that Jesus has perfectly defeated Satan totally. When Jesus died on the cross and rose from the dead, He conquered Satan. Further, redemption means that Jesus has bought us out of slavery, redeemed and ransomed us. Satan's strongholds can be attacked directly through prayer.

Before a lost person can be saved, Satan's stronghold needs to be torn down and this is accomplished through intercessory prayer. The conquest that Jesus has accomplished must be appropriated. It doesn't mean anything at all for the devil to be defeated 2,000 years ago if we don't awaken to that fact and claim the work of the cross. In prayer, an intercessor can exercise the faith of Calvary standing against Satan. The word of command that we have been given is the authority in His name to bind what He has bound and to loose what He has loosed (**Matthew 17:19, Mark 11:23**). In the Name of the Lord Jesus Christ, we can command obstacles and hindrances to the will of God to get out of the way. Before a lost person can believe, God wants us to cooperate by binding and loosing—rebuking and standing against Satan. Rebuking Satan on the lost person's behalf and binding him from that person's life is the role that an intercessor plays.

Ask God to bind Satan

Using the authority that we have in Christ to ask God specifically to bind the power of Satan (**Matthew 18:18; Mark 3:27**). We are called of God to be conquerors in spiritual warfare on this earth (**Ephesians 6:11-12**). James describes this warfare when he told us to submit ourselves to God and to resist the Devil so he will flee from us (**James 4:7**). This should not make us afraid. Truly it should give us great encouragement in our role as intercessors.

We have power in this warfare; the Lord Jesus Christ Himself is that power (**Ephesians 6:10**). We must stand our ground in this spiritual battle with the authority given us by God. Strongholds cannot stand against our authority when it is properly wielded (**2 Corinthians 10:4-5**). Just as a policeman can stop or move traffic by a gesture of his hand, so we, in Christ's name, command spiritual powers. Through prayer (in His name—by His authority) believers can command evil powers that bind the souls of people to release their captives. Remember that Satan is perfectly defeated and greater is He who is in us than the one that is in the world (**1 John 4:4**).

Through intercession, we claim the work of Calvary in the lost person's life. The blood of Jesus has atoned for the sins of the whole world. To pray in the name of Jesus is to claim everything that His work has purchased. The sins of an unsaved person have already been paid for by the blood of Jesus which has already been shed (**1 John 2:2, John 1:29**). Jesus has purchased the lost person. Remember that a person never goes to hell because of his sins (drinking, lying, fornicating, murdering, etc.). Rather, he is condemned because he has not believed in the name of the only begotten Son of God (**John 3:18**). Since Jesus has already paid for his redemption, we have the right to claim him in Jesus' name. **IN HIS NAME, THE INTERCESSOR HAS THE RIGHT TO CLAIM WHAT HIS BLOOD HAS PURCHASED!**

Toward the Savior. It is important to remember that a person does not come to Jesus except the Father draws him (**John 6:44**). It is through the Holy Spirit that the Father draws a person to the Savior. Jesus explained that it would be the work of the Holy Spirit to convict the world "*of sin, and of righteousness, and of judgment.*" (**John 16:13-14**). It is certainly appropriate for us to ask the Father to send the Holy Spirit to the unsaved person's heart to convict him and draw him. One can easily imagine the result in a lost person's thinking when he becomes conscious of his lostness and the coming judgment. Not only will the Holy Spirit bring the sense of conviction, He will do it in the light of calling attention to the Lord Jesus Christ.

Toward the Saints. In **Romans 10:1-3,8-13,** Paul gives the clear plan of salvation with the conclusion that *"whoever calls on the name of the Lord shall be saved."* Then, he poses a question in **v. 14**: viz., how can a person call on someone he has never heard about? Jesus instructed us to pray that God will send laborers into the harvest (**Matthew 9:35-38**). Keep praying that God will raise up someone to witness to the unsaved person. This is God's method. He prepares a sinner and he prepares a witness. In **Acts 8,** the eunuch was the prepared sinner and Philip was the prepared witness. In **Acts 10,** Cornelius was the prepared sinner who had been praying and fasting four days; Peter was the prepared witness. God's way is to bring together prepared sinners and prepared witnesses.

Through intercessory praying God moves to prepare the sinner. The intercessor needs to continue the cycle and ask God to prepare the witness that he will speak as he ought to speak and then give him an opportunity to share (**Colossians 4:12**). Don't be surprised if you become the witness God will use.

Let's pray for the lost

One very practical approach in praying for the lost is to choose five unsaved persons represented by the five fingers of your left hand and another five who will be represented by the fingers of your right hand. Pray for these every day following the ideas provided above. When one gets saved, replace that person with someone else. Know that it is the will of God that each of these persons be saved. Pray in the direction of Satan, in the direction of the Savior, and in the direction of the saints.

It is sad to note that there are saved people living with unsaved people under the same roof—often members of the same family and no one is praying for those lost people. Remember that if you are not praying for your children and grandchildren, no one else is. If you have lost your burden because of the pressures all around you and the pull of this earth, take this matter directly to the Father through the Lord Jesus Christ in the power of the Holy Spirit. He will deal with it and make things different!

Some years ago, it became clear to me that I needed to include a section in the prayer seminar on praying for the lost. Consequently, one of the last items that I teach is praying for the lost. On page 59 of the *Prayer Seminar Workbook*, I encourage the participants to become intercessors by organizing their praying according to the days of the week. On Saturday (page 60), pray for the sinners and seekers. The instruction provided is basically what is above. A lady in Boise, Idaho heard the teaching and decided to use the approach cited for her father, mother, and brother—who had all shown nothing but hostility toward Christianity. A short time later, she wrote to say that her mother and brother were gloriously saved and that she continued to pray for her father.

The work most needed is prayer work. Unless the prayer work is done, evangelism will make little difference. In fact, it is safe to conclude that it is possible to contact face to face every individual in a county or city with a gospel witness and see nothing happen if the prayer work is not done. **MAY THE HOLY SPIRIT CLEARLY TEACH EACH OF US THE NEEDED TRUTHS WHICH WILL RESULT IN OUR GIVING MUCH TIME TO PRAY FOR THE LOST!**

Study Seven

"Blessed is the nation whose God is the Lord."

Psalm 32:12

I love America! During these past few years, we have been privileged to travel to many nations conducting the prayer seminars. Each trip has been a blessing as we have observed beautiful places and beautiful people. We have been impressed by natural beauty. For example, the mountains in South Korea are unusually beautiful and 75% of the country is mountains! The South Koreans decorum is characterized by a sweet humility. Often I have thought, however, that the best part of a trip is getting home! I love America! My land! My people! To me, cold chills move over my body when I see Old Glory waving in the breeze outside our office building as it is doing as I write!

Crisis in America

Nevertheless, my nation is in need of healing that can only come from God—not education or the government. A few weeks ago, the news media announced that we have reached 258 million in our population. It seems to me Christians have become complacent and simply do not sense the crisis we are facing. Do you remember the 1960's and 70's? These are two decades that many would like not to remember! The futility that most of us felt toward the future was overwhelming as our cities burned. It seemed that everything that was nailed down came loose! Some declared that both God and the church were dead!

Christians awakened in late 70's and early 80's

In the late 70's and early 80's, Christians began to awaken and move to the forefront of influence. History affirms that the outcome of the 1980 elections was a direct result of their involvement. They registered voters and went to the polls. They not only voted for certain candidates; they voted against a number of Congressmen and Senators.

Since there were some changes which lessened the tension, the average Christian no longer feels concern. But conditions have deteriorated remarkably and the church continues to do business as usual. Christians are not even shocked by the immorality and violence all around us. Frankly, we have become desensitized by television! The looseness of morals in political, social, religious and business affairs no longer bothers us. Pornography in art exhibits is even paid for by government taxes and most Christians couldn't care less! The fall of several highly visible preachers makes the present danger of an anti-Christian backlash real indeed!

Does America really need healing or am I just shadow boxing? During the prayer seminar, we talk about current moral conditions in our country:

1. One of five Americans needs professional help because of emotional problems.
2. One of four babies born in America is born to an unwed mother.
3. There are three abortions a minute.
4. One of four homes with children is headed by a single parent.
5. Eight of each one hundred young people attempt suicide each year; eighteen a day succeed.
6. The divorce rate is 60%. 3.2 million are living together unmarried.
7. There are 22.6 million problem drinkers/alcoholics (18 million adults and 4.6 million children/youth). We do not have figures for other substance abusers, but the number is high.
8. There is one violent crime each 24 seconds.
9. There is one property crime each three seconds.
10. There is one rape each six minutes.
11. There is one murder each 28 minutes. Just this week, the news media announced that the United States is the murder capital of the world.
12. There are 2.5 million children abused annually. Three children die daily from abuse and neglect.
13. At the end of 1989, the number of federal and state prison inmates zoomed to a record 703,687, a 12.1 percent increase over 1988.
14 There are as many as three million homeless people in America—many with children living on the streets.
15. There are one million runaways.
16. Each eighteen seconds a woman is battered.

America needs healing

There are few families untouched by the problems listed above. Violent crime is up over 400 percent since 1963, child abuse is up 300 percent, federal prosecution of politicians has increased 470 percent, and the number of reported cases of

AIDS is up by 6000 percent since 1982. Even scores on college entrance exams taken by high school students have declined significantly since the early 60's. Yes, American needs healing.

What is wrong with the people in our nation that has turned "the land of the free and the home of the brave" into "the land of the spree and the home of the rave?" Could it be because we have left God out? We have "sown the wind" and "reaped a whirlwind" (**Hosea 8:7**), as did ancient Israel. **Every effort is being made to remove God completely from our national life! Where will it stop?**

Seven downward stages

In the book, **America: To Pray or Not to Pray,** author David Barton has postulated seven stages a nation goes through leading to eventual destruction by God. In the first stage, God convicts His people of their sins. Second, He warns them of sins. Third, He applies remedial judgment of sins committed. In the fourth stage, God withdraws His presence. In the fifth, He takes away the wall of protection and allows disasters to come upon His people. In the sixth stage, He gives His people over to sin, failure, and depravity. In the seventh stage, He destroys His people. Barton believes America is in the fifth stage.

Decadence, crime, violence, the recent onslaught of natural disasters, and an ecological system that is failing are signs God has turned His back on America as a nation. There is abundant evidence that God removed His wall of protection away from America sometime around 1963 when our Supreme Court ruled that prayer and Bible readings have no place in the schools.

What will turn the tide? **II Chronicles 7:14** is the text that tells us. It is spoken to Christians—"My people called **by My Name**" (which happened to believers at Antioch, Syria when they were called Christians first in Acts 11:26). There is an "**If. . . Then**" arrangement. God says to Christians "if" you do these things, "then" here is what I will do. Under "**IF**," He lists four things: (1) become humble which means dependence upon God—not ourselves or anyone else; (2) pray which means to ask in the sense of God's hand to move; (3) seek His face for worship; and (4) turn from sin. Under "**THEN**," He lists what He will do: (1) He will hear from Heaven—which is headquarters where all the resources that will ever be needed are in stock; (2) He will lift and remove the heavy load; and (3) He will heal the land. This is what will turn the tide for America or for any nation.

39

Remember that INTERCESSORS are literally "go-betweens"—standing between God and someone else or some circumstance. We need INTERCESSORS for America. Many of you are already intercessors and others want to become intercessors for our land. The assumption is that you will be on praying ground by having all sin confessed and forsaken and you are yielded to the Holy Spirit with Him in control—which is what Spirit-filled means. No believer can help turn our nation back to God unless he is clean before God. I would encourage you to get on your knees and ask God to make you a person He can use.

There are several directions for our praying for America. Pray toward God's people. Pray toward Satan.

Toward God's people

The key to bringing healing to a nation is in the hands of God's people. Therefore, we should direct our prayers that spiritual awakening and renewal will come to believers. Pray for conviction to come—which is the work of the Holy Spirit as He takes the Word of God and applies it. Pray that God's people will get into the Word and let God speak through His Word.

One major barrier to spiritual awakening is that few believers pay attention to the Word of God; most grossly ignore the Word. Pray that God's people will **repent** (change their minds about sin) and **confess** their specific sins by agreeing with God and saying the same thing about them that He says. Pray that God's people will be clean before Him—which will place them in a position of spiritual revival. BACK TO THE BIBLE IS A MUST FOR GOD'S PEOPLE!

Toward Satan

You can be sure that Satan is the force behind all that is happening to weaken and destroy America. He has mobilized his forces for the battle! If you have felt that everything biblical, Godly, pure and holy is under attack, that moral erosion is all about, that we seem to be losing a war but never really seeing the enemy, you are right! The principles and basis for our orderly society under God are indeed under systematic attack. It is evident in the schools, in the media, in literature, in the arts.

Secular humanism

There is a well-organized attack upon Biblical revelation and morality. Satan's tool is secular humanism that is promoted by a group known as the American Humanist Association. This movement is set against God and has permeated society with its spiritual poison. The humanists declare that belief in God is the highest form of self-deception. They think that the world would be better off without God. They believe that man is alone in this universe.

Don't think that secular humanism is a figment of fearful imagination invented by extreme, far-right fundamentalists. Here are the facts. In modern times, two astonishing documents have been drawn up, amply signed, publicly proclaimed, and then universally fulfilled—Humanist Manifesto I and Humanist Manifesto II. The first was published in 1933; the second in 1973. Both were printed in official publications of humanist organizations. Both were signed by a small number of incredibly influential people holding significant positions in all areas of society—science, politics, the arts, literature, the media, religion, philosophy and education.

By reading through these documents, you will gain stunning insight into the source of what is wrong throughout our society. You will see that the thrust of the well-organized attack upon Biblical revelation and morality mentioned earlier is delineated in these documents. Truly, these Manifestos are an attack upon the very conception of God. Once you understand the war against God, you will be in a position to enter into the battle through prayer with understanding and insight. As you read your daily newspaper, you will be amazed at the examples of the spiritual warfare in attacks against those things you hold dear.

Secular humanism is a religion

Although secular humanism claims to be against Biblical religion, it is in itself a religion. Secular humanism is cultured, educated, articulate, and deadly. Its adherents are in every segment of society. Its church is the public schools of America. Their pulpits are often the lecterns of college classrooms. Their interest is to cut the nerve of Christian commitment in students. Ultimately humanists are evangelists for a world free of God. They attack Christianity as a dangerous obstruction to truth and seek to eradicate the myths of Divine Providence.

It is imperative that prayer warriors become aware of what we need to stand against. A copy of the manifestos is available through the prayer seminar ministry. There are fifteen points in the 1933 Humanist Manifesto and seventeen in the 1973 document. A Christian should learn all the tenets and be on the alert for them. The tenets plainly advocate belief and practices that are explicitly contrary to Biblical teachings.

41

Summary of secular humanist's beliefs

A few of their beliefs are highlighted for your analysis:

1.**Creation and the Universe.** Humanism is directly based on evolution. The world was formed from chaos and is itself a chaos except as man's reason finds ways to organize it. There is no Creator. There is no divine purpose or plan.

2.**God.** There is no God. The 1973 Creed directly attacks the concept of God with its objective truth and binding morality. Since no master-Mind created the universe, there is no personal God who gives meaning to existence.

3.**Man.** Man is an "accident of chemistry." There is no higher authority than man who is more than capable of making his own decisions, mapping his own directions, choosing his own values and judging his own life. The mind of man is the key to a better world. *"Reason and intelligence are the most effective instruments that mankind possesses."* The complete realization of the human is in the here and now. Compassion and our working together for a humane world will bring progress. Man will be happy when he achieves economic well-being in a world of "shared human values." Happiness on this earth is all men can hope for since there is no heaven or hell. We strive for the good life here and now.

4.**Morality.** There is no absolute good or evil. Dogmatic or authoritarian religions that place revelation, God, ritual, or creed above human needs and experience do humanity a disservice. All acts are morally neutral, except for their influence on others for good or ill. Ethics is autonomous and situational, needing no theological sanction. Man can create a standard of right and wrong as he goes along, changing the rules whenever necessary to get rid of "old-fashioned ideas" like sexual continence. Toleration is a virtue. The good life mentioned above means the right to birth control, abortion, and divorce—which should be recognized. It is wrong to prohibit, by law or social sanction, sexual behavior between consenting adults. Individuals should be able to express their sexual proclivities and pursue their life-styles as they declare. Tolerance is demanded for premarital sex, extramarital sex, easy divorce, homosexuality—behavior once considered immoral or even illegal. Not only is abortion demanded, but so are euthanasia and the right to suicide.

A new world order is goal

Secular humanists have as their goal to establish a world-wide order along humanistic lines. Many of the signers were, or are, leaders in major educational organizations and are in the forefront of those who promote sexual freedom, the legalization of perversion, the legalization of drug use. Many are in high places of government. They make laws and influence laws. They write and publish the textbooks for schools and colleges. They control and program the media and influence the thought of our whole society with particular focus on our entire younger generation. They are out to make man the measure of everything. As the avowed enemies of Biblical revelation, they have succeeded in getting the Bible out of schools. Their goal is to remove any mention of God from our public lives.

The religion of humanism is widely taught in our schools while God's revelation in the Holy Scriptures is systematically restrained in the name of the separation of church and state. Constitutional safeguards have been turned against the Bible believer and now the clever, yet clearly stated goals of humanism as a religion, are clearly taught day after day. The success of the efforts is attested by the fact that vast numbers of people live by humanist values, although they may not attach the label to themselves. The tenets of secular humanism virtually have become the unofficial state religion of America and have been enforced by the courts wherever challenged. The biblical principles that guided the founding and development of America are rapidly being replaced by evolutionary secular humanism.

The success of secular humanism is astonishing and relatively few Christians seem to know or care that this is true. A recent fund-raising letter by Dr. Isaac Asimov, the current president of the American Humanist Association, gloats over this fact: *"We're on a roll and you can keep us there. The fundamentalists can't stop us now. Only a lack of support from you can bring our growth to a halt. But I'm confident you're with me. I'm sure you think it's high time the AHA realized its full potential. So let's go for it! Please make out a check right now, while this is in front of you."*

Few believe Genesis 1-11

As a result of the work of secular humanists, few are left even in Christianity who firmly believe in the historicity of the first eleven chapters of Genesis and special creation as opposed to evolution. Those who do are looked upon as ignorant, backward people. I have in my possession the California school code that states that evolution is to be taught as scientific fact. Since evolution is the very heart of secular humanism, think of the implications of that requirement. Why is it that the humanistic ideas have free course in our schools and any reference to God is not acceptable? Too long have we Christians forfeited our right to equal treatment under the law.

We will never win the war until we know where the battle is being fought. As born-again, Bible believers, we possess armaments and artillery that are supernatural. We will either use them or lose the war. *"The weapons of our warfare are not carnal, but mighty through God to pulling down of strongholds, casting down imagination and every high thing which exalts itself against God and bringing into captivity every thought to the obedience of Christ"* (**2 Corinthians 10:4-5**). Paul reminded the Christians in sinful Corinth that they possessed resources eclipsing anything the devil could muster. In **Ephesians 6:12**, he informed the Ephesian believers that *"We wrestle not against flesh and blood, but against principalities, against powers, against the rulers of the darkness of this world, against spiritual wickedness in high places."* Actually, this is a spiritual hierarchy of organization. Satan is not omniscient, omnipresent, or omnipotent—but he is organized. In order to do battle against him, Christians need to have on the whole armor of God. (**Ephesians 6:10-17**). After the armor is on, the first activity mentioned is prayer. The battle is fought in the place of prayer!

Toward governmental leaders

God has established three institutions: the home (**Genesis 2:18-25**), the government (**Genesis 9:1-17**) and the church (**Acts 2**). The Bible clearly teaches that we are to pray for those who have authority over us. This would include our civil leaders. Even when we cannot respect individuals in authority, we must respect their offices and pray for them. God Himself has given human rulers their authority (**Romans 13:1-7; 1 Peter 2:13-17**). Paul gives a specific order to pray for governmental authority (**1 Timothy 2:1-2**). Remember godless Nero was on the throne as Paul wrote this. Paul taught that God who is absolutely sovereign has placed each government official in his place.

One reason for such praying is that we will be able to live quiet (tranquillity arising from no outward strife) and peaceful (a calm attitude within) lives so that we can follow a manner of life which properly reverences God. Since Christians must be subject to rulers who have the power to persecute them, prayer is necessary to overrule them.

Prayer for the President

What should we pray? The following "Prayer for the President" written by Peter Marshall will give some ideas: *"We pray, Lord Jesus, for our President. We are deeply concerned that he may know the will of God, and that he may have the spiritual courage and grace to follow it. Deliver him, we pray, from all selfish considerations. Lift him above the claims of politics. Fill him with the Spirit of God that shall make him fearless to seek, to know, to do the right. Save him from the friends who, in the name of politics or even friendship, would persuade him from that holy path. Strengthen and empower his advisers. Bring them, too, to their knees in prayer. May their example and their influence spread, that we, in these United States, may yet have a government of men who know Thee, the Almighty God, as their Friend, and who place Thy will first in their lives as well as in their prayers. Hear and answer, we pray Thee, forgiving us all our unworthiness, cleansing us from every ignoble thought and unworthy ambition that we may be renewed in spirit and mind and heart, through Jesus Christ our Lord. Amen."*

I like that as an example! Pray that God will anoint President Clinton—who has testified that he is a born-again Christian. Pray for the members of his cabinet, our leaders in Congress and in other governmental positions—from the highest to the lowest.

Since 1988, our ministry has served as the Tennessee coordinator for the National Day of Prayer observed on the first Thursday in May each year. One day set aside annually is only a starting point. Why not encourage people to join with you in small groups for prayer according to **2 Chronicles 7:14?** When you are in prayer meetings and requests are made, focus on praying for our government calling out specific needs. Let us unite in prayer that God will send a spiritual awakening to the United States of America beginning in our hearts and spreading through the nation and the world.

It is not too late

Is it too late for America? I do not believe so. It is absolutely certain that when we do what God tells us to do that He will do what He said He will do. He will *"hear from Heaven, forgive our sins, and heal our land."* There is a prayer movement unparalleled in this century that is sweeping across America and around the world. Virtually thousands are giving themselves to prayer in the cities especially. A few years ago,

45

the Supreme Court ruled by an 8-1 vote in Westside Community schools v. Mergens that students in public secondary schools who wish to form religious clubs may have the same "equal access" to school facilities and privileges as students in other non-curriculum related activities. God's children have been praying for the Supreme Court whose decisions have closed God out of so much of our public life during the past thirty years. This is certainly a reminder that things can change. Let's commit ourselves afresh and anew to pray daily for the United States of America—your land and my land. Let us ask for God's blessings to rest upon us and give us a spiritual awakening that would sweep across our land beyond anything we have ever known. Where sin abounds, grace does much more abound! It is not too late!

Study Eight

"For this reason we also, since the day we heard it, do not cease to pray for you, and to ask that you may be filled with the knowledge of His will in all wisdom and spiritual understanding."

Colossians 1:9

One of my strongest desires is to minister to fellow believers through the prayer seminar ministry. It is not our intention to "receive;" we want to "give" to the end that believers will be strengthened in their own prayer lives and that prayer warriors will be enlisted. To accomplish this, the Holy Spirit spoke strongly to me during prayer toward the end of 1989 to provide in-depth Biblical studies in each of the elements of prayer. These twelve studies deal with intercession. Other in-depth studies are available through J. Gordon Henry Ministries on worship, how to study the Bible, and the Holy Spirit.

Praying for missionaries

Most of us are aware that we "ought" to become prayer warriors; most have not had needed instruction to be able to transfer the "oughtness" to reality. This study deals with INTERCESSION FOR MISSIONARIES which will be followed by a study on INTERCESSION FOR WORLD EVANGEL-IZATION.

Often when believers pray for missionaries, they feel that they are not being specific enough in their prayers which results in "God bless" or "God be with" prayers. The time spent in October 1989 conducting the prayer seminar with the Conservative Baptist missionaries serving in Italy afforded a very excellent opportunity for me to see that missionaries are human, too. Several shared some deep, personal feelings either in private conversation, the public meetings, or on the response form. Although I knew missionaries are human, rubbing shoulders with them on the field was good for my own understanding. While you may not know all needs, there are some specifics that are always in order.

Many of the ideas that I am sharing have come from missionaries themselves. One is Will Bruce who served for many years as a missionary to the Philippines and is associated with Overseas Missionary Fellowship. God gave me Will Bruce as a new friend several years ago when I learned that he has an intense desire to strengthen believers in their prayer lives. His list is not intended to be exhaustive, but is to get you started!

Unchangeable Variables

Missionaries face variables that include customs and culture, unfamiliar foods, climate, lack of privacy, language disparity, lack of adequate medical care, and few modern conveniences that the American has become accustomed. There is much to discourage and frustrate the missionary and his family. There is a difference in his western ways of doing things and what is done in his country. He must learn to be careful not to offend by thoughtlessly ignoring things that are important to those whom he is serving. There are often climate changes that tax the physical body such as intense heat coupled with high humidity, violent tropical storms, and rainy season deluges. Since many nationals live their lives in public, they expect the missionary to do the same. Finally, a lack of results can be extremely difficult to face since most missionaries arrived on the field expecting to "set the world on fire" for Jesus. Many variables that the missionary cannot control produce frustrations that can be defeating.

Pray that the missionary will be graciously flexible and able in very practical ways to worry about nothing and pray about everything (Philippians 4:6) as he looks to the Lord Jesus Christ. Pray for the missionary's heart to be filled with the supernatural love of Jesus (because natural love can break down and fail to meet the tests) which will prevent difficulties from bringing about hardness, impatience, sharpness of speech, anger, and even bitterness. Pray for God's love to be demonstrated through the missionary to fellow missionaries, to the believers with whom he labors, and to the unreached men, women, boys, and girls all around him.

Spiritual

The missionary needs to understand that he is engaged in spiritual warfare and needs to stand in the power of God (**Ephesians 6:10-18**). When a missionary goes to areas where Satan has held uncontested sway for centuries, it is important that the missionary have the spiritual resources to work. Satan does not meekly surrender even one inch of territory; rather, he will launch counterattacks and will fight to the last ditch. His primary attack is always on the mind. The missionary is in a spiritual battle and needs to understand fully what is happening. He needs to have on the whole armor of God that he will be able to stand against the "wiles" (specific stratagems for battle). Several have indicated that the daily pressures become so demanding that there is soon a neglect of the quiet time. Does that sound familiar?

Remember that the missionaries are not super-saints. *Pray that the missionary will maintain an attitude of humility (which is dependence upon God and not self). Pray that the missionary will renew his mind (Romans 12:2) with a daily time in the Word and in prayer.*

Pray that the missionary will stay in a position to qualify for God's looking his way—which is contriteness and trembling at His Word (Isaiah 66:2b). Pray that the missionary may enter into God's provision for rest and peace (Revelation 12:11, John 14:27, Hebrews 4:9). Pray for protection against Satan's attacks on the missionary's spirit. Intense powers of darkness make work difficult and slow.

Pray for his encouragement and strength to be given to break through the powers of darkness (Psalm 147:3, Deuteronomy 31:6). Pray that the missionary will resist Satan in the Name of Jesus (1 Peter 5:8-9, James 4:7). Pray that the missionary will take any accusation of Satan directly to his Defense Attorney to handle, the Lord Jesus Christ (1 John 2:1).

Brokenness necessary

It is necessary that the missionary live in brokenness that will produce the same attitude in national Christians (**Ephesians 4:15,16**). Witnessing and preaching in hardness will only harden the heart of the sinner; whereas brokenness and weeping will break hearts of stone (**Psalm 126:5-6**). If the missionary depends on his own strength, wisdom, and ability, Satan laughs because he recognizes only the power of God. It is vital that the missionary be clean and surrendered to the Holy Spirit—which is what "Spirit-filled" means (**Ephesians 5:18**). Pride of race, pride of face, pride of place (love of position) can easily creep in to neutralize the missionary's effectiveness. When self is in control, the ultimate result will be lack of consideration for others, attention-seeking, stubbornness, and the inability to see another's viewpoint. The gracious fruit of the Spirit must show in the life of the missionary. He must keep short accounts with both God and others. It is easy for the missionary to forget Jesus' words, "*without Me, you can do nothing*" *(John 15:5b).*

Pray that the missionary will learn to obey the instruction of Ephesians 5:18—"Be filled with the Spirit-"and will therefore walk in the Spirit and not in the flesh." Pray that the missionary will learn to submit his own desires and inclinations to God's Holy Spirit. Pray that the missionary will have the humility of Christ as described in Philippians 2:5-8.

Interpersonal relationships

The missionary's interpersonal relationships are all-important if God's work is to go forward unhindered. The oil of the Holy Spirit must be operative to assure that he gets along well with others—husband with wife, missionary with co-missionary, missionary with national Christian, missionary with national unbeliever. If relationships become strained, he needs to be honest and open with others; he must show real repentance and allow God to break his stubborn pride. It is no easier for a missionary to admit that he is wrong than it is for anyone else! It is so easy to stand against another instead of standing with him against the adversary.

Pray that the missionary will be surrendered to God and be sensitive to the prompting of the Holy Spirit in his interpersonal relationships.

Health

Both physical and emotional health are important. Excessive fatigue may cause depression or discouragement.

Pray that God will keep the missionary in that condition of health that will allow him to accomplish God's will and bring Him glory.

Safety

Travel on the mission field is often hazardous, whether by plane, bus, car, or on foot. Safety is an ongoing need.

Pray for safety in travel.

Family

A major factor is the missionary's spouse. God gives children to the missionary couple that need attention. Decisions made often have far-reaching effects on their lives as well as on their parents' lives. Missionaries need wisdom to train and teach their children in ways that are pleasing to God and that are in full accordance with His Word. Decisions, for example, related to education are often major ones.

Pray for the relationship of the husband and wife. Pray for the health of missionary children. Pray that parents may have wisdom in providing for their total needs. Pray for their education. Pray about the attitude of parents and children when it may become necessary for the children to be separated from the parents.

Quiet time

The missionary must take time to pray for every aspect of the work in which he is engaged if he is to experience the power needed. It is wise to begin the day praying specifically for the tasks of the day. Then, pray throughout the day as work is done.

Someone has said, "Better to do less work, if need be, in order to pray more; because work done by the rushing torrent of human energy will not save a single soul: Whereas work done in vital and unbroken contact with the living God will tell for all eternity."

Pray that the missionary will recognize and faithfully fulfill his part in prayer for the work to which God has called him. Pray that his motives will be right in everything that he does (James 4:3) which will place him into a position for answered prayer.

Conclusion

Prayer must be given a fresh, central place in our missionary support. Missionary endeavor must be based upon intercession if it is to have a solid foundation. It can only thrive and grow to the extent that it is cemented in the solid foundation of prayer. It is easy to become so wrapped up in our own frantic "goings" and "doings" that we never experience His marvelous moving. Prayer can be pushed into a corner in our daily schedules and lumped with things we intend to accomplish "if time permits." We therefore deprive the missionary of needed support. How wonderful and rewarding it would be if we could all live in the atmosphere of Paul's words, "*[we] do not cease to pray for you*" (**Ephesians 1:16**). We can if we will! May God grant to each of us a fresh realization of the fundamental importance of intercession for the missionaries. Through prayer, let's lift up the arms of missionaries on every battlefront as they proclaim the life-changing message of the Gospel of Jesus Christ.

Study Nine

"May God be gracious to us and make His face to shine upon us, that God's ways may be known on the earth, and salvation among all nations."

Psalm 67:1-2

"And as He taught them, He said, 'Is it not written, My house shall be called a house of prayer for all nations?'"

Mark 11:17

What have been your thoughts as you have studied the area of intercessory praying? Are you clear on what intercession is? An intercessor is one who stands between God and someone or some circumstance. There is a need to **spend time** in prayer **seeking God's face**—which is worship including adoration and praise for Who God is. There is a need to spend time in prayer **seeking God's cleansing**—which is confession of specific sins. There is a need to spend time in prayer in expressing gratitude—thanksgiving for what the hand of God has bestowed including physical, material, spiritual, and people blessings. There is a need to spend time in prayer **praying for ourselves**—which is petition for personal needs, direction, strength. Including all these in daily meaningful prayer takes time and effort. Then, there is a need to spend time in prayer **praying for others**—which is intercession and which makes a tremendous difference since GOD MOVES WHEN HIS CHILDREN PRAY. In the light of the potential to effect eternity, one could easily conclude that the greatest bulk of prayer time should be in the area of intercession. What do you think?

World evangelization

The subject for this study is WORLD EVANGELIZATION. **World evangelization is the process by which the Lord Jesus Christ is revealed to every person and each is offered the Gift of Eternal Life.** Do you have the world on your heart? Few do. Most are very provincial in outlook and concern. There are 5.6 billion people on earth today; two out of three have never heard the name "Jesus" in a saving sense one time. Is this because God is partial and has favorites? Are the little children wrong when they sing "Jesus died for all the children of the world, red and yellow, black and white, They're all precious in His sight?" No, God does not have favorites. You will never meet a person that God does not love. The little children are not wrong!

Years ago, someone shared that a Chinese translation of **John 3:16** reads "For God so loved THE PEOPLE OF the world." I like that translation, don't you? Man was created for His glory and it would please His heart and bring Him joy for every person to acknowledge Him and respond to His love. But this can never happen until people learn about Him—Who He is, what He has done for their redemption, and what He wants for their lives. A person can never call on one He has never heard about.

There are at least 240 nations and territories. Out of this number, 110 have closed their borders to missionaries. God does not need a visa. There is no border that He cannot penetrate. We can be assured as God's children, in obedience, begin to pray, He will move! Consider what has happened in Eastern Europe in the past few months! The Berlin wall is no more!

What can an individual believer do to have a part in reaching the world as a prayer warrior? As noted in the last study dealing with praying for missionaries, I will not have the final word in a single study. We can at least get started and begin to build a base for intercession for the world. After each individual sees that there is something that he can do, he can then share his understanding with others in his local church.

John 17: primary passage

John 17 is the primary passage that can get us started. In the prayer seminar we stress that **John 13, 14, 15, 16, and 17** is a passage every believer should master. These chapters contain the final words of Jesus prior to His returning Home to the Father—His final instructions to his disciples. Two subjects are covered: (1) the Holy Spirit and (2) Prayer. Jesus knew that the Holy Spirit would be One just like He was to the disciples. He wanted them to understand that they would never be alone (**John 14:18).** He wanted them to know, also, that they could do something now that they had never done before—go directly to the Father in prayer asking things in His name that the Father would be glorified in the Son when answers came (**John 14:13**).

After His specific instructions, our Lord's Prayer is then given in **John 17**. The prayer reveals the great love that Jesus has for His followers as we carry out His commands to evangelize the world. Again and again, He prays "*Father,* *glorify Yourself!"* **Everything we could desire for the people of the world and everything God wants to be in them and do for them is spoken in the prayer, "Father, Glorify Your name in (whatever individuals, locations, areas of influence for which we pray)" or "by (defeating Satan, calling and preparing workers, opening doors, pulling down strongholds)."**

Listen to what the Holy Spirit is saying to you as you read: Christ *"lifted up His eyes to heaven, and said, 'Father the hour is come; glorify Thy Son, that Thy Son also may glorify Thee: As Thou hast given Him authority over all flesh, that He should give eternal life to as many as Thou hast given Him. And this is life eternal, that they might know Thee, the only true God, and Jesus Christ whom Thou hast sent'"* (**John 17:1-3**). Jesus sought to please and glorify the Father, not Himself; we need to follow His example.

Jesus then prayed that those who receive Him be kept from the evil one in His name, and sanctified in His truth (**John 17:4-17**). Jesus revealed that He has sent us into the world to show the world who He is as His glory is revealed in us. Then He prayed that believers be one in Christ, as He is one in the Father, that the world will believe that the Father sent the Son into the world to redeem the world— *"that the world may know that Thou hast sent Me, and has loved them, as Thou hast loved Me"* (**John 17:18-23**). When the body of Christ is in agreement and we are one in Him, in unity with the Father, Son, Holy Spirit, and each other, there is no force in the world that can withstand such power and love. In fact, only the demonstration of such love for one another can ultimately defeat Satan and reach the unsaved. The gates of hell cannot prevail against His Church as we move forward to share the Gospel—the Good News of the Lord Jesus Christ—His birth, life, death, and resurrection for the sins of mankind.

Through intercessory prayer for the world, we can unite with Jesus in His prayer for the world and with Him as He intercedes for the lost. We can **pray that the name of the Lord will be glorified in all the earth.** We can pray that believers be one in Christ! We can pray to prepare the way for evangelization— which will virtually break up the soil so that it is ready for the Seed—the Word of God!

Laborers

The question was raised earlier as to why so many in the world have not heard about Jesus. The answer is really not difficult to understand. In **Matthew 9:35-38**, **Luke 10:2**, and **John 4:35**, Jesus emphasized to His disciples that it was harvest time; the fields were white. He cautioned them not to say that the harvest was four months away; rather the fields were then white. When it is harvest time, laborers are required to gather the harvest before it perishes in the field.

In **Romans 10:1-3, 8-13**, Paul shares how to be saved clearly and succinctly. This is the passage that we use to teach believers how to bring others to Christ. The conclusion is that the person who believes that God has raised Jesus from the dead and is willing to acknowledge that He is Lord will be saved by asking Jesus to save him. Beautiful! What follows, however, is often overlooked. In verse 14, Paul notes that a person cannot call on the Lord for salvation if he has never heard about Him. Therefore, there is a need for a laborer who will share the Gospel. Can't you see why Jesus spent valuable teaching time telling His followers how to get laborers for the harvest? The only way that Jesus gave us is to pray. How disobedient and rebellious we are in following His command! If you record every prayer prayed today and there is one for laborers, I will be very surprised. We simply don't obey the Lord and pray for laborers.

The starting point in intercession for world evangelization is simply asking God to send out laborers. The scope of our concern should be the entire world. In the prayer seminar, we use the lesson of bi-focal glasses through which a person can see clearly both at a distance and nearby. Through the top part, one can see clearly at a distance; through the bottom part, clearly up close. We need praying that sees across the ocean and we need praying that sees across the street. We use a log illustration in the prayer seminar. There is a heavy log to be lifted and you come along. There are ten already lifting—one on the light end and one on the heavy end and you really want to help. Which end of the log would you go to help? The aim is to emphasize that nine out of ten Christian workers work with 6% of the world's population; one out of ten works with 94%. Can we reach the world like that? The answer is "No!" By the way, before going to either end of the log, the believer should first go to the Superintendent of the project—our Lord—and ask Him to which end of the log to go and then obey!

God's people

One does not need to spend much time reading John 17 until

it becomes obvious that a major focus of the praying of Jesus was on these whom He was given out of the world. He said that He manifested the Father's name which is to say that He revealed the Father's nature and character to the end that "they have come to know that everything Thou hast given Me is from Thee" (v. 7). Then He gave His followers a mandate to reveal (manifest) Him to the world. He knew their success was dependent on their union with Him, not on their abilities or methods of evangelization. Using His *example and keeping unbroken fellowship with Him, we can strength*en one another for the task that has been given us by praying for one another around the world daily.

Let us pray that His followers be kept in His name (v. 11) and be kept from the evil one (v. 15). Pray that His followers will live out before a lost world so that people can see who He really is and that heir witness will be strong and effective. Pray that they be set apart for God and His holy purposes which iswhat Jesus meant when He prayed that believers would be "sanctified in truth and sent into the world as He was sent."

revealed the Father's nature and character to the end that "they have come to know that everything Thou hast given Me is from Thee" (v. 7). Then He gave His followers a mandate to reveal (manifest) Him to the world. He knew their success was dependent on their union with Him, not on their abilities or methods of evangelization. Using His *example and keeping unbroken fellowship with Him, we can strength*en one another for the task that has been given us by praying for one another around the world daily.

Let us pray that His followers be kept in His name (v. 11) and be kept from the evil one (v. 15). Pray that His followers will live out before a lost world so that people can see who He really is and that heir witness will be strong and effective. Pray that they be set apart for God and His holy purposes which iswhat Jesus meant when He prayed that believers would be "sanctified in truth and sent into the world as He was sent."

There is no substitute for personal holiness in the life of a Christian. Our witness has little effect if we are not being conformed to His image. Unsanctified living leads to a tarnished witness. Pray that wherever God's people are that they will love one another. Jesus taught plainly that it is through the love that believers have for one another that the world will be reached.

e is no substitute for personal holiness in the life of a Christian. Our witness has little effect if we are not being conformed to His image. Unsanctified living leads to a tarnished witness. Pray that wherever God's people are that they will love one another. Jesus taught plainly that it is through the love that believers have for one another that the world will be reached.

Satan

Prayer touches hell. When it does, it looks toward Satan. That is warfare. We are in a war, not on a holiday or picnic.

Many believers today are becoming aware that there is a spiritual war going on. Satan wants to have free course that will end in all mankind's bowing before him in worship. He is not omniscient, omnipotent, nor omnipresent. Rather, he is organized and has a plethora of workers. The hierarchy of his organization is clearly outlined in **Ephesians 6:12**. There are four layers of power depicted in the satanic hierarchy of organization.

Satan is the head, the first layer of power. Then he has key officers (the generals), the second layer of power. There is a third layer that would be middle-level officers, such as the majors, the captains, and such; Finally, the lowest level would be the demons and one-third of the angels. but he has his key officers such as the "prince of Persia" (**Daniel 10**). There is another layer listed and finally the lowest level—which I presume is filled by demons and one-third of the angels. Through united efforts, Satan works to defeat the individual Christian, to keep the Gospel from being spread and made available, and to blind the eyes of those who do hear. In order to make a difference, the believer must know where the battle is being fought. Remember this truth: "*I will never win the war if I do not know where the battle is being fought!*" The battle is fought in the place of prayer (**Ephesians 6:**18).

the lowest level—which I presume is filled by demons and one-third of the angels. Through united efforts, Satan works to defeat the individual Christian, to keep the Gospel from being spread and made available, and to blind the eyes of those who do hear. In order to make a difference, the believer must know where the battle is being fought. Remember this truth: "*I will never win the war if I do not know where the battle is being fought!*" The battle is fought in the place of prayer (**Ephesians 6:**18).

According to **Daniel 10**, there are officers of Satan assigned over geographic territories. Although I do not know what their job description is, I do know that they are powerful and that they are not "flesh and blood." In Daniel's day, the Prince of Persia hindered the answer to Daniel's prayer from getting to Daniel for twenty-one days. Amazing!

It seems to me that a believer can go on the offensive against the princes and things will begin to happen. As we attack, Satan, his cohorts, and his organization can be rendered ineffective through prayer; he is already defeated and it is through prayer that we establish his defeat. Those who followed historically the praying for Eastern Europe know that some believers even went to the Berlin Wall. They stood against the powers of evil in the name of the Lord Jesus Christ and His shed blood, and asked God to tear the wall down! That was only a few years ago and look at what has happened!

We are to occupy until He comes (Luke 19:13). As Christians, we are to rule and reign in Him. We have the authority to ask anything in His name. Asking that His name be glorified in all the earth is a prayer of surrender of ourselves and our methods of evangelization to Him as His will is done. We take ground from Satan. Through prayer, we till the soil to receive the precious Seed—the Word of God.

A global prayer strategy

For several years, prayer leaders in the world have been seeking a Global Prayer Strategy that can unite Christians around the world in prayer in a way that has never happened before. God answered the pleas of these leaders and has moved them to a simple, Biblically-sound strategy that is already in place having been launched in July 1989. The Father showed the prayer leaders how to have united, unending prayer of agreement around the clock and around the world through two simple ideas: (1) Every morning as the sun rises in every country and time zone around the world, Christians rise to meet the SON and pray for world evangelization and (2) Every Christian using **John 17** as the guide to pray for God's glory to cover all the earth and bring all mankind into union and relationship with Jesus Christ.

Each believer can begin to pray for world evangelization. Let every sunrise remind you to pray for His glory to be over all the earth. When you do, you will be joining with Christians around the world united in unending prayer until He returns! Do you see what a difference this will make?

During a prayer seminar, each participant is encouraged to choose a nation to pray for specifically. As you focus on the nation, pray for the needed laborers to carry the Gospel to everyone in that nation Then, pray for God's people in that country. Ask God to defeat Satan in that area. This is something all of us can do. Why don't you do that?

Work

You will remember that prayer touches earth, looks toward people/circumstances and that is WORK (*Prayer Seminar Workbook*, page 8). In order to accomplish intercession, a believer must first of all be willing to set aside the time needed for intercession for world evangelization. The two big words are **DISCIPLINE** and **PRIORITY**. Only you can make the decision as to how you will use your life for the Lord Jesus Christ. The flesh does not like to do prayer work! The devil puts anyone on his hit list who even thinks about becoming a prayer warrior! Someone noted that "*we have enthusiastically equipped enough unanointed saints.*" In conclusion, we come back to exhort: first become clean before God and then surrender the control seat to the Holy Spirit. It will then be that you will be in a position to be the prayer warrior that will make a difference! I hope you will!

Study Ten

"I exhort therefore, that, first of all, supplications, prayers, intercessions, and giving of thanks, be made for all men; for kings, and for all that are in authority; that we may lead a quiet and peaceable life in all godliness and honesty."

II Timothy 2:1-2

"O that one might plead for a man with God, as a man pleadeth for his neighbor."

Job 16:21

We continue our study dealing with various aspects of intercession. Intercession is prayer as work. The focus is earth—people and circumstances. The sense of intercession is asking God's hand to move. When Paul shared insights into his own prayer life, it is clear that much time and energy were given to praying for others. Moreover, he described his intercession as *"striving in prayer"* (**Romans 15:30; Colossians 2:12, 4:12**) which means to the point of exhaustion. Who among us has learned to pray with such intensity? Probably most of us don't do enough prayer work in a year to make a butterfly tired!

Prayer is the "greater work"

Intercessory prayer is work, and without prayer there is no work. Intense prayer was made by the Jerusalem Church for Peter *"without ceasing"* (**Acts 12:5**). Dr. R. A. Torrey translates *"without ceasing"* as literally meaning *"stretched-out-edly"* which pictures the soul on the stretch of earnest, intense desire. Oswald Chambers said: *"Prayer does not fit us for greater works; prayer is the greater work."* It is noteworthy that the **GREATER WORKS STATEMENT,** a part of the Upper Room discourse which took place a few hours before the crucifixion, is clearly in the context of prayer (**John 14:12-14**). When the Lord Jesus Christ was on earth, He had limited Himself to a physical body that performed in time and space. Now that He is in Heaven, He has no such limitation. Thus, E. M. Bounds concluded: *"Prayer is not the foe of work; it does not paralyze activity. It works mightily; prayer itself is the greatest work."* Watchman Nee observed: *"Let us understand that the church's noblest work, the greatest task she could ever undertake, is to be the outlet of God's will. For the church to be*

61

the outlet of God's will is for her to pray." Do you understand that prayer is work—which means the expenditure of energy?

Believers sleep on

"While the bridegroom tarried, they all slumbered and slept" **(Matthew 25:5).** You will note in your Bible studies that both tares and wheat are allowed to grow together until there will be a separation day. We all know that it is probable that there are many unsaved persons who are baptized members of local churches. The sad part is that **"all"** slumbered and slept. There were ten virgins—five saved and five unsaved—but "all" slumbered and slept. When our Lord went into the Garden of Gethsemane in great agony of soul, He was accompanied by eleven disciples. It appears that all eleven slept! Could it be that a local church could be a sleeping giant instead of a force engaged in prayer work? The results of other efforts affirm that such is true in many local assemblies. Intercessory prayer is work! We must WORK FOR THE NIGHT IS COMING, WHEN MAN'S WORK IS DONE!

In this study, we will focus on some practical suggestions to use in intercession. In the next study, we will focus on Paul. We will look at specific requests that he made, the prayers that came in response to the requests, and the answers. Once you see the accounts of God's moving in Paul's life related to the prayer support he received, you will see the importance of praying today. The final study will deal with intercession for pastor-teachers.

My friend, the late Armin Gesswein, has wisely noted that *"worship is before work and all His works are done in the spirit of worship."* Further, he points out that *"There are many churchgoers, but few worshipers, because there are few prayers!"* You and I should be willing to examine how prayer lives and made any needed adjustments in our work as intercessors.

Where to begin

Intercession literally means standing between God and people/circumstances. Remember that the word is from two Latin words that together mean **"a go between."** Intercession is seeking God's blessings for those around us. In reality, it is likely that the beginning point in intercession will focus on the needs (spiritual, physical, material, and emotional) of relatives, friends, and fellow church members. Some of these are lost; others are Christians. A recurring prayer request on the response envelope that we use to close a prayer seminar is for loved ones who are Christians who are living beneath the resources and privileges freely available to God's children. A recent request illustrates the often expressed concern: *"Pray for my children who have made a profession, but who are not living for the Lord."* I can only believe that it is not only right, but obligatory, for believers to pray for those close around us. If we don't pray for our children regularly, we can be fairly sure that no one else is; if we are not praying for our grandchildren, no one else is!

Pray from a prayer list

   To guide intercession, it is vitally important to pray from a prayer list. List the people/circumstances for which you want to pray and record the date. There are a number of ways to do this. You might want to organize your prayer list with these designations: **family** (immediate family and other relatives), **friends** (relationships outside your immediate family—you might want to break this category down into saved and lost), **government** (local, state, and national), **ministries** (church staff, church services, missionaries, and parachurch groups such as J. Gordon Henry Ministries). Present their needs to God by name. One rule of thumb is to **pray for them exactly as you would want them to pray for you.** During the prayer seminar, we discuss organizing praying according to the days of the week (pages 59-60, *Prayer Seminar Workbook*).

   We make available for a contribution to the prayer seminar ministry, the *A-C-T-S Prayer Diary,* which is arranged to organize daily intercession. Although there are other resources, none are better than this particular tool.

Pray from the Word

   One way to pray for others is to be alert to the Holy Spirit's guidance as you read your Bible each day for identification of prayer promises you can pray. One person counted more than 7,000 promises in the Bible. A promise is a pledge to do, or not do, what is specified. A promise is only as good as the one who has made the promise. We can be sure that we can depend upon the promises God has made. A few weeks ago, He impressed **Psalm 80:18** as a verse to pray for several in my family: *"So will not we go back from Thee: quicken us, and we will call upon Thy name."* A father could pray **1 Chronicles 29:19** for his son: *"And give unto [name] my son, a perfect (sincere) heart to keep Thy commandments, Thy testimonies, and Thy statutes."* Remember that a promise has to be CLAIMED BY FAITH to receive the blessing promised from God. As you read your Bible daily —with pen in hand—make it a point to **LEARN, CLAIM,** and **PRAY the promises!** Don't just make a file of them. Time cannot erase the promises of God; circumstances cannot dim them; wicked rulers cannot destroy them. You and I can effectively nullify them if we don't claim them!

Pray the Scriptures as prayers

The **Bible** contains ready-made prayers. As you memorize the Word of God, you will find that the Holy Spirit often brings such prayers to mind as you pray for others. One example of a prayer that can be prayed for someone is a passage that is used in the prayer seminar, **1 Chronicles 4:10:** *"O that You would bless* [name] *indeed and enlarge his coast* [give him more responsibility], *and that Your hand would be with him, and that You would keep him from evil that it may not grieve him."* The conclusion is: **"And God granted him that which he requested."** This is a marvelous prayer to pray for your pastor or a missionary. Another verse from the prayer seminar is **1 Thessalonians 5:23** that could be directed toward a person for whom you are praying: *"And the very God of peace sanctify* [name] *wholly; and I pray God* [his/her] *whole spirit and soul and body be preserved blameless unto the coming of our Lord Jesus Christ. Faithful is He that calls* [him/her], *who also will do it."*

When you pray for other Christians (based on **Ephesians 1:16-19**), you can pray, *"Father, in the name of Jesus, would you give* [specific name] *a spirit of revelation? Please open their eyes that they might know what is the hope of your calling, the joy of being a Christian, and to know what is your inheritance and your power that is working in them."* What would happen if we begin to pray **Ephesians 3:14-16** for church leaders, teachers, and brothers and sisters in Christ? *"Lord, I pray that you would strengthen them with might by Thy Spirit in the inner man, that Christ may be at home in their hearts, that they may be able to comprehend the love of Christ."*

Comprehending the love of Christ would surely make a difference! Make specific requests for those for whom you are praying. Here are examples: **Bill:** Please show him what drinking will do to his life. **Dad:** Give him wisdom in the job decision he is making. **Mary:** Help her as she shares Christ with her roommate. Through intercession, we can focus the power of God on another person or on a specific situation. When a fellow believer is going through a trial or difficulty and the devil is oppressing him, pray that God would open his eyes so that he might know the power of the Holy Spirit that works in him. If one is difficult (a little cantankerous and touchy), pray that God's love may abound in that person **(Philippians 1:9-11).**

Once you begin to pray the Scriptures directed toward those for whom you are praying, you will always be glad that you do. Remember, the Holy Spirit can bring words to the mind that have been put there by hearing, reading, studying, memorizing, and meditating on the Word of God. It is unlikely He will do so if the Word is not hidden in your heart. Our goal should be to **Pray the Word!** As well as **Preach/Teach the Word!** Then don't forget to record the answers in your prayer diary. Reviewing a running prayer journal will constantly remind you that you serve a prayer-answering God! What an encouragement that will be!

Study Eleven

"Now I urge you, brethren, by our Lord Jesus Christ and by the love of the Spirit to strive together with me in your prayers to God for me."

Romans 15:30

We have dealt with various aspects of intercessory praying. The work that is needed before any other work is prayer work. Intercession has been defined and various elements of intercession have been illustrated. There has been an effort to provide Biblical studies to the end that believers will be encouraged and strengthened in their commitment and practice of intercessory praying. We desire to enlist prayer warriors.

What good is it to pray for someone else and circumstances? Does prayer make a difference? Won't God do it anyway whether we pray or not? Is there real power in intercessory prayer? Think about the church prayer meeting. What kinds of requests should be made on behalf of someone else?

Surprisingly, the only NT writer to ask for prayer by others on his behalf was Paul (unless someone else wrote Hebrews). Paul believed beyond a shadow of doubt in the effectiveness of intercessory prayer. Much can be learned from his personal experience.

The church at Rome

Paul urged the church at Rome to strive together with him in prayer. Ken Taylor's paraphrase is quite graphic: *"Will you be my prayer partners? For the Lord Jesus Christ's sake, and because of your love for me—given to you by the Holy Spirit— pray much with me for my work. Pray that I will be protected in Jerusalem from those who are not Christians. Pray also that the Christians there will be willing to accept the money I am bringing them. Then I will be able to come to you with a happy heart by the will of God, and we can refresh each other"* (**Romans 15:30-32 LB**). I like that, but it doesn't reflect the intensity of the Greek.

"Strive together with me" is a picture of the apostle and the believers at Rome standing side by side on the spiritual battlefront, waging warfare for the Gospel. It is laboring to the point of exhaustion. Through such praying, the Christians at Rome could join Paul in the work he was doing for the Lord.

The prayers of God's people can move to any point in the world energizing God's servants for their tasks. Think of that! God's design is to allow His children participation in His spiritual purposes for the earth! Entrance into prayer is unrestricted. The most humble and uneducated of God's people can pray. Distances and difficulties cannot deny the opportunity to pray.

By looking at Paul's specific prayer requests and what happened in Paul's life, we can test the effectiveness of intercessory prayer. There were three objects of concern.

1. Deliverance in Jerusalem (v 31). Paul urged the Roman believers to pray that he might *"be delivered from those who are disobedient in Judea."* His worst fears were realized when he was attacked by his enemies in the Temple a little over a week after his arrival in Jerusalem (**Acts 21:27**). He was rescued by Roman soldiers. Why did the mob not succeed in their wicked design? Roman Christians were praying that he be delivered as Paul requested! Even then, an assassination plot was concocted; his enemies did not give up easily! But a young boy overheard the plotters (**Acts 23:16**). The young boy was Paul's nephew who reported what he heard to his Uncle Paul. It is rather amazing that the Roman centurion would believe a boy's tale! He did and literally employed hundreds of soldiers to get Paul out of Jerusalem and down to Caesarea on the Sea (**Acts 23:23**). Further, the Lord Himself stood by Paul on the night immediately following his arrest to tell him: *"Take courage, for as you have solemnly witnessed to My cause at Jerusalem, so you must witness at Rome also"* (**Acts 23:11**).

2. Acceptance in Jerusalem (v.31). When Paul wrote to the Roman believers, he was concerned that his efforts in raising a relief offering for the saints in Jerusalem among Gentile believers not be misunderstood or rejected. It seems that his relations with the Jerusalem church were tenuous at best and that he had strong opponents over the requirement of circumcision (**Acts 15:12**). The Church at Rome prayed. What happened? The Holy Spirit moved Luke to note that which otherwise would have been taken for granted: *"And when we had come to Jerusalem, the brethren received us gladly"* (**Acts 21:17**). God answered the intercession of the Roman believers!

xxxxn study eleven, the emphasis of our study on intercession was answers to the prayer requests that Paul made. **3. Visit to Rome** (v 32). Paul's third request for prayer was that he might *"come to [them] in joy by the will of God and find refreshing rest in [their] company."* The way that Paul got to Rome was probably not the way he visualized. He anticipated another missionary journey—this time to Rome and to Spain. God had a ticket to Rome waiting for Paul at Caesarea. A pagan society provided the passage to Rome for God's missionary. As Roman Christians were praying for Paul's request, God was moving on his behalf. A terrible storm developed en route and an angel of the Lord told Paul: "*Do not be afraid, Paul; you must stand before Caesar; and behold, God has granted you all those who are sailing with you*" (**Acts 27:24**). After fourteen days in the storm, the ship ran aground and broke up, but Paul and all the others were cast up on the island in Malta—every life was spared.

Cold and wet, Paul helped the others gather firewood so that they could dry out and be warmed. A snake was in the bundle of sticks he carried to the fire and sank its fangs into Paul's hand. The natives expected him to die and concluded he was a murderer and that some kind of unseen power must have determined he would not escape! Paul simply shook it off and was unharmed! There certainly was unseen power in what was happening; it was the power of God in cooperation with prayer. God's people were praying and God was at work. Nothing could keep him from Rome!

Intercessory prayer is praying on behalf of God's purposes in the earth and in accordance with God's will. It may be impossible to explain how God incorporates the prayers of His people in doing His work, but the sovereign God has made it possible.

Churches at Corinth, Ephesus, Colossae, and Thessalonica

Paul earnestly sought the prayers of God's people because he believed this to be a part of God's provision for the meeting of his situation. Not only did he ask the Roman Christians to pray, but he expressed the same view when he wrote to the church at Corinth that they were "*also joining in helping us through your prayers, that thanks may be given by many persons on our behalf for the favor bestowed on us through the prayers of many*" (**2 Corinthians 1:11**). He called to the remembrance of Ephesian believers the importance of their prayer on behalf of others, saying, "*With all prayer and petition pray at all times in the Spirit, and with this in view, be on the alert with all perseverance and petition for all the saints*" (**Ephesians 6:18**). Paul wanted the Ephesian Christians to be sensitive to the needs of other Christians and to be exercised in prayer on behalf of them. Then he made a specific request for himself, that he would both know what to say on behalf of the gospel and then have the courage to say it (**Ephesians 6:20**). This request is notable in that his concern was not for a change in circumstances as an "*ambassador in chains*"—but for faithfulness in those very circumstances. Is there any doubt as to whether God answered?

Colossians is likewise a letter written from imprisonment in which Paul encouraged believers to devote themselves to prayer. His specific request was that they would be "*praying at the same time for us as well, that God may open up to us a door for the Word, so that we may speak forth the mystery of Christ, for which I have also been imprisoned*" (**Colossians 4:3**). Paul told the Thessalonians he needed their prayers in order to carry out his ministry: "*Pray for us that the Word of the Lord may spread rapidly*" (**2 Thessalonians 2:1**). He also believed their prayers were needed that he be delivered from "perverse and evil men."

Our call to intercession

How many times some believers say: "*Please pray for me!*" with a ring of earnestness? Sometimes those words throb with all the pent-up agony of a burdened soul. It is profitable to pray for someone else. There is real power in intercessory prayer. One need only track Paul's life to see how that he made his requests known to fellow believers at one point. Later, there are written accounts to demonstrate that God moved to meet his needs.

For whom are you praying? We can be sure that if we are not praying for our loved ones by name that nobody else is! If you have grown weary in your intercession or if you have become careless—and the Holy Spirit has spoken to you through the Word of God that has been shared—don't waste time in regret. Agree that your prayerlessness is sin, that you are guilty and ask for forgiveness and cleansing. "*Father, You want me to pray for others. I agree with you that I have sinned by my failure to do what you want me to do. I've changed my mind about my prayerlessness and acknowledge that my neglect is sin. I say the same thing that you are saying. Please forgive and cleanse me.*"

On the authority of God's Word (1 John 1:9), we can claim forgiveness and cleansing: then, yield control afresh and anew to the Holy Spirit. Allow Him to sit on the control seat of your life. He will help you form a prayer list. Begin to pray knowing that the sovereign God has ordained prayer as the tool to get His work done and that God works only in concert with the praying of His people!

Paul not only wanted God's people to pray for him, but he often interceded for others. It is undeniably true that involvement in intercessory prayer has an effect on the one who prays. The church at Antioch had a continuing prayer meeting in which Paul was a participant (**Acts 13:1-3**). A few others were there, but not many. Barnabas, Simeon, Lucius of Cyrene and Manaen, who had been brought up with Herod the Tetrarch, joined Paul in *"ministering to the Lord"* through praying and fasting. The object of their concern must have been the further extension of the gospel, especially to the Gentiles. It was then that the Holy Spirit commanded that Barnabas and Paul be separated to the work of ministry to regions beyond. It very well may be that you will want to either renew or begin a commitment to join with other believers in intercessory prayer. God moves when His people pray!

Study Twelve

"I beseech you brothers that you strive together with me in your prayers to God for me."

Romans 15:30

In study eleven, the emphasis of our study on intercession was answers to the prayer requests that Paul made. The sequence was (1) Paul's request; (2) prayer support given; and (3) reports that illustrated that God answered. Paul did not hesitate to ask for prayer support. **Pastors need prayer, too!** Most pastors, however, are not well prayed for at all! When the pastor stands in the pulpit, he is considerably well on his own as far as prayer support is concerned!

Daily praying

During the prayer seminar, there is an effort to provide ideas for the participants to organize their prayers lives. My suggestion is that the days of the week be used as dividers for prayer with specific emphases on each day. Nevertheless, there are some areas that require daily prayer—one's family and one's pastor and his family. What a difference it makes when there is prayer support for the pastor.

Prayer is work—which demands energy and effort. **Charles Spurgeon** knew that. The power of God was in his ministry at the Metropolitan Tabernacle in London and he was often asked the secret of the blessings. His reply was simply *"My people pray for me."* At one period during his ministry, there were 400 men praying in a downstairs auditorium while their pastor preached upstairs. And the power of God came! He knew that prayer support was the secret of his success—not his own competencies or abilities.

In the people gifts that God gave the church listed in **Ephesians 4**, the one that makes a difference in countless lives today is the pastor-teacher. As you pray for your pastor, don't forget to thank God for this spiritual gift to you, your family, your church, and your community. His task is to be a player-coach who equips the believers to do the work of the ministry. As goes the pastor, so goes the church. A church will never move to a level of spirituality beyond the level of their pastor's spirituality. In order to provide the leadership that is needed, he must have the power of God. He needs prayer, too! He needs ongoing, sustained prayer support. Everyday you should be praying for your pastor-teacher. Be specific in your intercession.

In preparation for your prayer support, you need to remember that as Elijah, your pastor is "*a man of like passion such as we*" (**James 5:16-18**). This means the pastor is an ordinary person. We forget sometimes that we have this treasure in earthen vessels; but such is the case. Study Paul's prayers to gain fuel for your prayers. An example is his prayer for the Colossians: "*For this reason we also, since the day we heard it, do not cease to pray for you, and to ask that you may be filled with the knowledge of His will in all wisdom and spiritual understanding; that you may have a walk worthy of the Lord, fully pleasing Him, being fruitful in every good work and increasing in the knowledge of God; strengthened with all might, according to His glorious power, for all patience and longsuffering with joy; giving thanks to the Father who has qualified us to be partakers of the inheritance of the saints in the light. He has delivered us from the power of darkness and translated us into the kingdom of the Son of His love, in whom we have redemption through His blood, the forgiveness of sins*" (**Colossians 1:9-14 NKJV**). How many specific prayer items can you identify in this prayer? Write them down in numerical order. You will be surprised at the insight that this will give as you think through what you should pray for your pastor. Other Pauline prayers are **Ephesians 1:15-23; 2:14-21** (one of my favorites); **Philippians 1:9-11; 2 Thessalonians 1:11-12; 2 Corinthians 1:9-11**).

Be systematic and organized

As you read the long list of prayer suggestions that follow, remember that your praying will be more productive if it is systematic and organized. ayer suggestions that follow, remember that your praying needs to be systematic and organized. You need not think that the list is ex**hausti**ve and all-inclusive; neither is it intended to be used entirely daily. You must allow the Holy Spirit to guide you in your prayer emphases as you pray daily for your pastor. Remember, prayer is work—which means that time and energy are required. Unless you "go to work" in prayer as you would in your work, it will not make much difference.

The Word of God and prayer

One of the pastor's hardest tasks is to keep spiritually

fresh. Although much can be said about many prayer needs, it is obvious from Acts 6 that the pastors need to be freed from responsibilities and work that can be done by others in order to devote themselves to prayer and the Word of God. Some pastors turn out all the lights, close all the doors, and perform time-consuming chores that not only drain their energies, but rob them of the time needed to be in the Word and in prayer. How tragic!

Prayer for the pastor's Bible study

It was not until 1977 that I was confronted with the reality that my time in the Word of God was to get a message to preach, not for my own food and guidance. For twenty-four years as a pastor, I really neglected the Word of God. Although I did my best to preach the Word, my time in the Word was to get a Biblical message together. Pray that your pastor will love the Word. He needs to hear, read, study, memorize, and meditate on the Word for his own life. After I began to get into the Word daily for spiritual food, my life changed! Whereas I had to struggle to have something to say, now I have more to say than I have time to say it!

Pray for the pastor's prayer life

A prevailing subterfuge of Satan is to bring into the pastor's psychic a pervasive feeling that he has things he needs to be doing which results in his cutting short his prayer time. Pray that the pastor will understand that this is simply Satan's attack and that he will have victory. Pray that he will make prayer a priority in his daily life—Jesus did! The pastor will never be in a position to provide help for his people in the most neglected area of all—prayer—unless he himself has a prayer life and understands prayer power. He will never win the war if he does not know where the battle is being fought; the battle is fought in prayer (the first activity mentioned in Ephesians 6:18 after a person has his armor on)!

Dependence on God

Humility means dependence on God and not on our own strengths and abilities. One reason that many pastors do not have the power of God is that they are depending on their own power. This problem is compounded when the pastor becomes an educated pastor and has earned a few degrees! It is further compounded when the pastor has a pleasant personality and a pleasing physical appearance. You can tell how important some think they are by observing their walk and talk! No pastor will ever be worth much to the Kingdom who has not come to the point of complete dependence on God. Pray he will have a servant's heart.

Contrite means brokenness. God has promised to look to the person who is contrite and who trembles at His Word (Isaiah 66:2b). Pray that the pastor will walk in true brokenness. The pastor needs a teachable spirit. He must have a servant's heart. Pray that pastor will be so completely dependent upon God that he will not be devastated by negative criticism or failures. He must know that he is to fear God, not man. After all, the pastor is working for God—not a congregation of people. Pray to this end!

Spirit-filled living

Pray that the pastor will be clean before God and be in a position for the Holy Spirit to sit in the control seat of his life. The pastor needs love, joy, peace, patience, kindness, goodness, faithfulness, gentleness, and self-control (Galatians 5:22-23). The only way for these traits to become active in his life is to allow the Holy Spirit who is resident to be president! Love is the fruit Spirit and out of love comes the other eight qualities. Circumstances, people, things, and worry often rob a believer of his joy. Unconfessed sin robs the believer of his joy.

Pray that the pastor will develop a single mind (which is only on Christ), a submissive mind (which causes him to put Christ and others before himself), a spiritual mind (which is more interested in heavenly than earthly things), and a secure mind (which comes when one is surrendered to God who guards us and gives us peace.

When the pastor loses his joy, he will not worship, witness, work, walk, or war very well. Remember what happened to David when for one year he lived with unconfessed sin (**Psalm 51 and 32**)? Pray that the pastor will have true joy. Only then will he be in a position to teach transgressors God's ways, which will result in conversions (**Psalm 51:12-13**).

Pray that the pastor will show Calvary love in all interpersonal relationships! Pray that your pastor will move right into the middle of **1 Corinthians 13** and stay for the duration! Pray that he will keep his eyes on the Lord!

Spiritual warfare

As is true of the Christian life, the ministry is spiritual warfare—not just a job or profession. Pastors are subject to the three-fold Satanic temptation of the lust of the flesh, the lust of the eyes, and the pride of life (**1 John 2:16**) just as is every other believer. Because he is a spiritual leader, you can be sure that Satan has your pastor on his hit list and will entice him to sin. To nullify his spiritual influence would be a big victory for Satan. Pray that the pastor will have power and safety to overcome temptations. Pray that he will resist moral temptation—that his words, actions, and thoughts will be Godly.

Self-control

Among the qualities listed in **Galatians 5:22-23** is self-control that is love triumphing over selfish inclinations. A pastor must be self-disciplined to use his time effectively. Ask God to help him be able to say "no" when he needs to do so, as well as "yes" as appropriate. Pray that the Holy Spirit will make him sensitive in these matters and that he will always be keenly aware of the effects of his actions on the testimony of the Lord, the Church, and his family. Pray that the pastor will deal with anything in his own life that is not in line with who he is and Whom he serves.

Priorities

A pastor needs to know that the order of his priorities should be God first, family second, and ministry third. If a pastor isn't cautious, his work will be first, God second, and last family. Often Satan attacks a pastor's family to bring him to defeat. A pastor and his family live a "fish-bowl" life-style. You should pray for his role as a husband and father. Pray for his family as well. Pray that the pastor will be able to maintain a scriptural family seeking God's wisdom for the nurture and discipline of his children. Pray he will provide adequate spiritual leadership for each member of his family.

Health

Your pastor needs a measure of health and physical stamina to serve the Lord and people. Pray that he will guard his health with proper food, exercise, rest, and relaxation. Pray for safety as he travels. Pray that he will learn God's lessons from any illness that might come his way and that his health be restored in God's good time.

His ministry

There are various dimensions involved in serving as a pastor-teacher including preaching, teaching, administering, and counseling. A congregation will reflect one day the interests of a pastor; therefore, pray that his message and his methods will be completely Biblical in every aspect.

Preach the Word

The pastor is to *"preach the Word"* (**2 Timothy 4:2**). He does not need to spend his time catching people up on the latest news or analyzing the latest philosophies. He needs to use the Word (not human ideas and wisdom) to explain the Word! Pray that pastor will receive his message from Heaven and will then deliver it to the congregation unchanged and without compromise. With boldness, tenderness and love, pray that he will provide the whole counsel of God.

Pray that the pastor will confront sin as he proclaims repentance toward God and faith toward the Lord Jesus Christ (**Acts 20:27**). Pray that he will stay on target and not go off on tangents. Pray that his messages will be Christ-centered and Christ-exalting. Pray that he will make the personal preparation needed to preach with power.

Win souls

A pastor is to *"do the work of an evangelist"* (**2 Timothy 4:5**). The fruit of a Christian is another Christian (**Luke 13:6-9**). How sad it is when the pastor-teacher is barren. It is unlikely that a local church will bring many people to the Lord Jesus Christ if the pastor himself is not winning souls. The one need that determines whether he will be fruitful is a burdened heart for the unsaved. Pray that the pastor will be an exemplar of **Psalm 126:5-6**. When a pastor develops a burden for souls that is placed in the proper perspective of a goal to bring one person a week to Christ (as an example), he will often go far beyond his goal.

Summary

No matter how much you provide for your pastor (salary, benefits, housing), there must be prayer support above all. No matter how much you encourage him with your words and works, his effectiveness will be a reflection of the prayer support that he has from his people. It is only through earnest, strategic prayer that you can ever really help him be an effective pastor-teacher. Every pastor-teacher needs prayer for his personal

It is amazing how hearts are knit together (**Colossians 2:2**) when there is mutual praying—pastor praying for his people and the people praying for their pastor! Let's do it! needs, for spiritual wisdom and power, for his family, and for his ministry.

The sovereign God has ordained prayer as the tool to get His work done. God works only in concert with the praying of His people. Your pastor deserves daily prayer support! Pastors need prayer, too! Will you determine now to give it?

Study Thirteen

Samuel Chadwick, one of God's great servants in past years, maintained that Satan's greatest aim is to destroy our prayer lives. Satan is not afraid of prayerless study, prayerless work, or prayerless religion, but he trembles when we pray. If Chadwick was correct, and any student of the Bible knows that he is, then we have a real problem today. If there is any part of our church life that seems to be in trouble, it is the **prayer meeting**. In fact, an increasing number of churches, for all practical purposes, have disbanded the prayer meeting altogether.

Most believers will agree that the prayer meeting is the "power house" of the church. The only problem is that the prayer meeting is the least attended meeting in the church venue. Charles Spurgeon captured the common attitude in churches when he chose the title of his famous exhortation to prayer— **Only a Prayer Meeting**. He raised a question that still needs to be raised. Why do many members fail to grasp the momentous significance of the prayer meeting?

The principle of shared prayer between ordinary believers was supremely established by the Lord Jesus Christ when He said, "Again I say to you that if two of you agree on earth concerning anything that they ask, it will be done for them by My Father in heaven. For where two or three are gathered together in My name, I am there in the midst of them" (**Matthew 18:19-20**). The context is the local church. When the Lord uttered these words, He was instructing the disciples about church affairs.

The church at prayer

You will remember that the only thing Jesus left to continue His work on earth was **a praying church**. The early believers who gathered on the Mount of Olives on the day of His ascension were excited as He spoke to them. They wanted details of His promised return. In a sense, His disciples asked Jesus for a prophecy conference (**Acts 1**), but He did not give them one. Instead, Jesus sent them to a prayer meeting that you can read about in **Acts 1**. It was after a ten-day prayer meeting that the Holy Spirit came on the day of Pentecost. He provided the power to make their witnessing effective. Following what appears to be no more than a ten-minute preaching service led by Peter, who was using the keys of the kingdom that Jesus had promised would be His, around 3,000 Jewish people trusted Christ as Savior and Lord. Following an extended period of prayer, the church was empowered to minister effectively. The same power is available today. We need the church to return to the prayer meeting if we want to see similar results. Much prayer, much power; some prayer, some prayer; no prayer, no power.

We can only wonder what will happen when the church returned to the prayer meeting in a serious commitment and undertaking. Before this can come about, however, it is obvious that Christians must get a handle on their own prayer lives. Since 1980, my ministry has been going up and down the land (and in other nations) calling people to prayer through a six-hour prayer seminar. The focus of the prayer seminar is to help an individual Christian get a handle on his/her prayer life and become a prayer warrior, not on corporate praying. Once a believer develops his own personal, regular, daily time with God, he will bring power to the church prayer meeting. If he does not have a personal prayer life, his presence at the prayer meeting will be ineffective.

A praying church

In many ways, the church is in captivity and bondage, as was ancient Israel. One principle that is illustrated in the biblical accounts is that God's people need to ask for His hand to move on our behalf. The Bible, in a sense, is the record of crying out to the Lord for deliverance and receiving His blessing. It was when the children of Israel sighed by reason of their bondage in Egypt that their cry came up to God. Only when they cried out to Him, did He deliver and bless them.

Moses prayed, and cried out earnestly. What was the result? The waters of the Red Sea parted before the people. Elijah cried out for the rain, and it came. Throughout church history, the same is true. All the awakenings and reformations began with souls awakening to cry out for God's mercies through concerted, sustained prayer. Every great blessing in the life of a church, as in the life of an individual Christian, is obtained through prayer.

The worst mistake that an individual Christian can make is to neglect his prayer life because he cannot receive any great blessing without prayer. Without prayer, he lacks any deep experience with God and there will be no significant spiritual interventions in his life. What is true of individuals is true also of churches. No prayer, no blessing; limited prayer, limited blessing. We need to understand the special privileges and rules of church prayer meetings laid out in the Bible. To that end, the following studies will focus on the prayer meeting when God's children gather corporately to become intercessors, doing the prayer work that God requires. My prayer is that the studies will restore a great sense of the importance of the prayer meeting in the hearts of all readers.

Again, we need to remember that there is power in agreement when people, even two persons, come together for the church prayer meeting. There is special power in the prayer of God's people when they are assembled together. The promise is made to the smallest plural company possible—two people. The Lord's utterances are infallible. When He says, "two people," He means "two people." When two people meet together and "agree" on what they ask, a wonderful thing will happen because this is the form of prayer to which He attached a special promise. He will answer their request. What does the word "agree" mean? In the Greek, it is a word of enormous significance.

The Greek word for the verb *agree* is *sumphoneo*, from which we get our English word *symphony*. It means "to sound together in harmony" and refers primarily to musical instruments. When Jesus said when two agree, the sense is "when any two of you sound together." The word is used to describe instruments playing harmoniously together. When two believers "harmonize" about a matter in the unity of the Spirit, unity of desire, and unity of prayer, it sounds like the music of a beautiful symphony in the ears of God. God the Father will surely ratify and answer such a request. Why? Because where even two or three pray together in Jesus' name, Jesus Himself will be there praying with them, agreeing with them, and amen-ing their prayer. Further study on **Matthew 18:19-20** is provided in **Study Seventeen**.

In other places in the New Testament, the word is used to describe the way in which two people verbally strike a bargain. An example is in the parable of the vineyard recorded in **Matthew 20**. When the keeper of the vineyard "agrees" with the laborers, it is the word used. They bartered, and then came to an agreement audibly.

When used in prayer, this word refers to prayers spoken aloud, audible prayer, not silent prayer. During the recent work in South Africa, there were occasions when different people prayer aloud at the same time. When this is the format, there can be no intelligent agreement. In the "sounding together" denoted by the word "agree," one prays and the others follow silent, winging those desires heavenward along with the one who prays aloud. The sense is that the Lord's people subordinate themselves one to another, and lead one another in prayer. Upon this type of praying, there is the unique favor of God. The aim is to be at one in the things for which we are praying.

As we understand more clearly the biblical teachings on corporate prayer, we will see that they can be carried out in the church prayer meeting. It is time to put the prayer meeting back into the life of our churches. The hour is late and the needs are great. It is time to act.

Pastors praying

As is true in other aspects of the church, the pastor, himself, must be a praying person. Most believers need help in their prayer lives—help that is not being given. Often pastors share privately with me that the weakest part of their ministries and their Christian lives is in the area of prayer. This is a need that must be addressed.

A few years ago, a pastor stood at the close of a prayer seminar to address his people. He began to weep and confessed to his people that for months and months he had neglected praying for his flock. The church congregation was growing rapidly. A major building program was underway. He shared that every time he started to pray that he thought of pressing matters than needed his attention. During the prayer seminar, the Holy Spirit had worked in his heart to enable him to see himself as God saw him. He said to His people, "You have a new pastor, now."

Many pastors say, "This prayer seminar was for me. It was what I needed at this time in my ministry."

I want to share a letter received from Richard W. LaFountain, pastor, The Pitman Alliance Church, Crafton and Oakcrest Avenues, Pitmen, New Jersey 08071, following a prayer seminar in his church a few years ago.

Dear Dr. Henry:

What a joy it was to have you in our church this March 10th! Our hungering hearts were fed from the Word an inspired and challenged by your remarks. We were especially pleased to see the good turn out in the afternoon and evenings sessions. May this be the beginning of what the Lord longs to do in this place!

We will be following up on the seminar. Our elders will have a prayer day on April 6 down at the shore. Each of them will be allowed to invite just one other man to join them in this "Time of refreshing in the presence of the Lord." We will begin with breakfast at the home of our head elder, and then proceed to the shore to arrive by 10 a.m. The day will be structured with instructional times, interspersed with times of STILLNESS, WORSHIP, THANKSGIVING, AUTHORITY POSITIONS, and SURRENDER that will lead us into times of INTERCESSION, READING, and EXHORTA-TION.

I personally enjoyed the seminar and it confirmed many of the things that I have been sharing with the congregation regarding prayer. Over the past two years, the Lord has led me into a more ordered prayer life based on **Proverbs 25:28**: "He that has no rule over his own spirit is like a city that is broken down, and without walls."

I sense that the majority of Christians today have NO WALLS, that is, no personal discipline of the mind and body before the Lord. This spiritual neglect has made us vulnerable to ever invasion of the enemy on every side both in our personal lives, as well as in the church. We are cities without walls of protection. Is it any wonder that the enemy reaps havoc in our churches! With this realization, I sought the Lord to ORDER my steps in prayer. In the Word, there are many patterns of prayer, as you well know. My particular discipline grows out of my study of the Scripture of the Lord Jesus Christ's commands for our prayers.

PREPARATION
BE STILL—Psalm 46:10; Isaiah 30:15
WORSHIP—Psalm 27:4
CONFESSION—Psalm 66:18
THANKSGIVING—Psalm 95:2; Hebrews 13:15
DEAL WITH THE DEVIL—Ephesians 6:10-18
DEAL WITH SURRENCER—Romans 12:1-2; Ephesians 4:18

INTERCESSION
SALVATION OF SOULS—Psalm 2:8
PEOPLE'S NEEDS—Matthew 18:18-19
HEALING: BODY/MIND—James 5:13-16; 1 John 3:8b
CHURCH MINISTRIES—Matthew 16:18
MISSIONS—Ephesians 6:19-20; 2 Thessalonians 3:1
GOVERNMENTS—1 Timothy 2:1-2,4

I have found that if I have not entered into the presence of God in true heart preparation, then I am not ready to do the work of intercession. The greatest enemy of my prayer life is hurry! Because of my own need of discipline of mind, the Lord led me to use a three minute egg timer as I pray. Sounds crazy, doesn't it? Yet it has done wonders to order my mind and heart in prayer. I have determined in the beginning to spend not less than three minutes on each of these areas in prayer. God has commanded each one. Are they not worthy three minutes of my focused attention? Three times twelve steps is thirty-six minutes of dedicated praying. I have found that three minutes is not enough! In most cases, it barely gets me started, so I just flip the timer for another three minutes, and another when necessary.

The real value in this prayer schedule is the consciousness that it has developed a pattern in prayer beginning with WORSHIP, then CONFESSION, and finally INTERCESSION. Prayer is a joyous time of fellowship with the Lord. I look forward to these times of refreshing. I need these times of BASKING, instead of always ASKING.

One of the richest experiences we have had here at the Pitman church is a four-hour prayer concert in which this prayer pattern was translated into rooms of the church as stations of prayer. There was a room decorated and dedicated to each aspect of this prayer discipline. There was a QUIET PLACE where a person could go to be alone in silence before the Lord until his heart was still in God's presence. There was the WORSHIP ROOM where chorus and hymn books, and cassette worship tapes with earphones were provided for praise. There was a BURDEN ROOM where one could go to pray for specific burdens from the Lord or to help another person pray over a burden. There was the MISSIONS ROOM with maps, missionary pictures, prayer letters, and the like. There was the WAR ROOM where we put on the armor of God and stood against the enemy with our sword and shield. And on and on it goes!

People who never come to a prayer meeting came and most stayed the full four hours and when it was done said, "Let's do it again." They wanted more! It was a way to teach the discipline of intercessory prayer providing enough variety to keep a person very awake and involved the full time. I'll enclose the outline of the evening as we planned it. Feel free to share it, adapt it, or use any ideas you might glean from it.

I encourage busy people to spend the PREPARATION part of intercession in the early part of the day. Eighteen to twenty minutes basking in the presence of God keeps you conscious of His presence all day. Then for the intercessory time, use your lunch hour, at least twenty minutes. Or, as I like to do, I set my watch to beep on the hour every hour and mandate a discipline mind and heart to stop whatever I am doing for three minutes of intercession on one of the areas of God's concern.

For those who find it difficult (even I carry a 3x5 card with the twelve steps outlined), I encourage them to divide their prayer in three distinct part; WORSHIP, CONFESSION, INTERCESSION and that each time they pray in the day they use the three minute timer technique spending one minute in praise, one minute in confession, and one minute in intercession. It moves people from NOTHING to something of discipline in prayer, and begins to build the WALL and repair the breach (**Ezekiel 22:30**).

May the Lord daily strengthen and use you!

Sincerely yours,

Signed by the pastor

THE MAIN THING IS TO KEEP THE MAIN THING THE MAIN THING. Prayer is one of the five emphases of the early church. It is time to revive the prayer meeting to unleash the power that prayer brings.

Study Fourteen

Needed: Spiritual renewal in America

For national welfare: "Righteousness exalts a nation, but sin is a reproach to any people" (**Proverbs 14:34**). "The wicked shall be turned into hell, and all the nations that forget God" (**Psalm 9:17**). "And that, knowing the time, that now it is high time to awake out of sleep: for now is our salvation nearer than when we believed. The night is far spent, the day is at hand: let us therefore cast off the works of darkness, and let us put on the armor of light" (**Romans 13:11-12**). "Therefore, He says, Awake, you who sleep, Arise from the dead, and Christ will give you light. See then that you walk circumspectly, not as fools but as wise, redeeming the time, because the days are evil. Therefore do not be unwise, but understand what the will of the Lord is" (**Ephesians 5:14-17**).

The face of America is changing at an accelerated rate. Christians were incensed a few years ago when a theologian declared that God is dead and expressed concern for the spiritual condition of our nation. Many began to pray and to return to the Word. The concern did not last, however, and soon we were drifting along once more. 9/11 moved us to understand the need for God and for His blessings upon us as a people. Hope was expressed that once again we were moving back toward God and the principles detailed in His Word. In a sense, the sleeping giant simply awakened briefly, turned over, and went back to sleep. The moral erosion continues. For many, morality is relative and there are no absolutes to guide behavior.

Almost daily, examples in the media remind Christians that a spiritual war is being waged in the United States. November 2003 will likely go down in history as the month when one of the most serious attacks has come on America, precipitated internally by the judicial branch of our government, not externally by our nation's enemies.

On Sunday, November 23, 2003, our home church pastor, Jack Barrett (Forest Baptist Church, Forest VA) spoke on the crisis facing America using **Romans 1:18-32** as his text. Using a decision by the Massachusetts' Supreme Court mandating that commonwealth's legislative body accommodate gay marriages within the next six months. He noted that a moral vacuum has been created and that Christians have sat on the sidelines with the attitude that we don't want to be judgmental. He pointed out that many of our prevailing attitudes simply do not square with the Word of God. Speaking from **Romans 1**, Pastor Jack encouraged His flock to respond in four ways:

1. With common sense (**vv 26-27**). Many of the actions being taken in America are unnatural in the light of **Genesis 1:27-28**.
2. With genuine concern (**vv 26-32**). There are consequences to sin as is illustrated by David's agony described in **Psalm 51** and **Psalm 32**. We need to be concerned for people who are blind and have gone astray. Jesus is our model. We need to reach out with love to bring sinners to a saving knowledge of the Lord Jesus Christ remembering Jesus died for sinners. We cannot put our heads in the sand. Otherwise, we are approving those who practice ungodliness and are headed for eternal death.
3. With compassion. We must love sinners into the kingdom of God. Lifestyles change when one becomes a Christian and begins to walk with God. This is our hope.
4. As a community, we must get engaged and involved. It is time to use our voice in our society and with our elected officials.

What can Christians do to make a difference? What can you do? We must pray for spiritual renewal in America; then we must put legs to our prayers and be willing to take steps that will make a difference. The Word of God provides the insights that are needed for effective praying and for influencing the nation. It is time to act before the door is closed and there is no opportunity to stand for Christ and His Word in a free nation.

Biblical background

God speaks to His children out of His Word. Read and consider each reference that follows. When you understand the implications of the text for your life, check it off. This exercise will provide heart preparation to engage in spiritual warfare for the nation.

- ❑ **2 Chronicles 7:14**
- ❑ **2 Chronicles 20:3-37**
- ❑ **1 Timothy 2:1-4**
- ❑ **Joel 1 & 2**
- ❑ **Ezra 8:21-23**
- ❑ **Jonah 3:5-10**

Get on praying ground

Begin with worship. Praise the Lord. It is good to sing praises to our God, for He is gracious and a song of praise is appropriate. 'You are worthy, O Lord, to receive glory and honor and power, for You created all things, and by Your will they exist, and were created" (**Revelation 4:11**).

✓ Praise God as the Lord of history who is working out His plan according to His perfect will.
✓ Praise the Lord that He is the God of revival, who revives His people in answer to their prayers in His perfect timing.

Heart searching. "Search me, O God, and know my heart; try me and know my thoughts; and see if there are any wicked ways in me, and lead me in the way everlasting" (**Psalm 139:23-24**). Do not try to search your own heart. Just pray honestly and expect God to search you and convict you as needed.

✓ Pray for yourself seeking a right attitude toward God, others, and our nation.

Confession. As you think about your life in the light of God's way, you may already know something you need to confess or may discern that the Holy Spirit has brought conviction regarding specific sins or failures to confront. Some common items to confess might be as follows:

✓ Let us confess that we tend to be self-reliant and fail to trust God totally;
✓ Let us confess that our commitment to follow God's way and to do His work is often half-hearted;
✓ Let us confess indifference and failure to pray regularly for our national and local government.

Accept His forgiveness. Confession brings forgiveness and cleansing (**1 John 1:9**) but we must be willing to receive the forgiveness. Take a moment to reflect on His forgiveness, thank Him, and receive this wonderful gift. You are now on praying ground.

Thanksgiving. Thank God for the privilege to worship Him freely in our country today following the dictates of our own hearts and consciences.

Pray for Christians—"His people called by His name"

1. That Christians may become sensitive to sin and freely confess and forsake all unrighteousness (**Proverbs 28:13**);
2. That God's children may repent and return to loving God with all their hearts (**Matthew 22:37-38**, **Revelation 2:1-7**);
3. That Christians may humble themselves and forsake the spirit of pride (**2 Chronicles 7:14**; **I Peter 5:5-8**);
4. That the spirit of prayer and humble repentance might be poured out upon all Christians;
5. That a mighty spiritual awakening will sweep through the entire Christian community regardless of denominational affiliation;
6. That Christians may be cleansed and live in holiness;
7. That His church will repent and be restored to wholly following the Lord in renewed love and devotion to Him, to fellow believers, to our neighbors, and to all people;
8. That the revived church may renew its efforts to fulfill the Great Commission with fresh vigor.

Pray for Christian families

1. That they will realize afresh the power of God's grace for reconciliation, as needed, resulting in harmonious living producing a sense of security and love to maximize growth and development;
2. That entire families may learn to find agreement with Christ in patient, united prayer (**Matthew 18:15-20**);
3. That Christian parents may learn to pray like Noah, whose intercession saved his entire family from perishing with a godless society in the flood.

Pray for our nation

1. Pray that Christians will be inspired by the Holy Spirit to join in prayer for our nation on a daily basis;
2. Admit to God that we need His mercy and divine intervention on our behalf as a nation;
3. Ask God to restore righteousness and wisdom to those who govern (**2 Samuel 23:3-4**, **Proverbs 29:2**, and **Daniel 2:20-22**;

4. Pray for the President, Vice-President, members of the Supreme Court, U. S. Senators, your Congressman, state senators, state representatives that they may come to know God and perform their duties with honor to ensure we have good government that can be blessed by God;
5. Pray that the influence of Christian political leaders will be felt in a positive and strong fashion;
6. Pray for the families of the Christian political leaders who are under attack with very direct pressure to compromise their biblically based convictions and standards;
7. Pray for the salvation of government leaders;
8. Pray that the Bible study and prayer groups in our national and state capitols will continue to be a light and an inspiration to those who participate and that their co-workers will be blessed by the overflow coming from the groups.

Pray for your church

1. Ask God to reveal what part your church is to take in the working out of His divine purpose for our nation;
2. Pray for your pastor and the leadership that they may provide needed guidance to the congregation;
3. Pray that the members of your congregation will be knitted together in love and become a mighty force to stand for righteousness in the nation starting locally.

Actions to take

Offer yourself to God for any part He way assign to you in His plan to restore the United States to the moral ground set forth in the Declaration of Independence and the Constitution in the light of **Proverbs 29:18; Matthew 6:10**.

Contact your governmental leaders and your local media. Write personal letters to the president, members of Congress, members of the state legislature. Tell them that you are praying for them. Let them know your specific concerns. Remember the following points as you compose your message:

➤ Use words that are gracious and Christlike;
➤ State specifically what you are concerned about; (Pastor Jack suggested to say plainly: "This really breaks my heart. I'm afraid of the consequences for my family and my nation."

- State what you want done about it;
- Explain why you want something done now and how it affects you and your family in an immediate way.
- Keep the message as concise and brief as possible, preferably on one page.

Chronicles Commission

Doorkeeper Suzy Kauffmann (Mrs. Howard), Atlanta, suggested that it is time for Christians who know the **Great Commission (Matthew 28:19-20)** commit themselves, first, to a **Chronicles Commission (2 Chronicles 7:14)**. I agree wholeheartedly. Until the requisites of this text are met, we are unlikely to fulfill the Great Commission. She asked, "Do you think we, as Christians, are commissioned by God to obey the passage if we want our land healed?" Yes, I do think that and see the value to calling each **Doorkeeper** to accept the **Chronicles Commission**. It is high time to awake and to act!

Study Fifteen

"Wilt Thou not revive us again: that Thy people may rejoice in Thee?" (**Psalm 85:6**)

During the past few months, the Holy Spirit has turned my thoughts more and more to the spiritual and moral decline so rampant in our culture. How can this be in a society that has churches on every corner? The answer appears to be that the church, in a real sense, has lost its influence. The church's greatest need is the need for revival. We need a revived church. Consequently, I have been alert in reading the Word of God and during prayer times to promptings of the Holy Spirit to give attention to seeking God for revival—in my own life and ministry and in the body of Christ.

Someone has observed that the church in the world today is much like a sleeping giant. What would happen if the giant would awaken? When revival comes, the giant will not only stir and awaken, but will begin to move with dynamic power and spiritual impact. A primary image of the church is the Body of Christ. Imagine the Body of Christ moving throughout the world with unified purpose and spiritual power. Perhaps that concept is too staggering for us to grasp. If this is so, think in terms of your own local congregation. Imagine what would happen if all alike were intent on seeing the will of God done on earth as it is in Heaven. Imagine what would happen if there were no sleeping Christians and no backslidden believers. Add the power of the Holy Spirit unleashed as Jesus revealed in **Acts 1:8**. The Greek word for power is *dunamis*, literally *dynamite* power—the same kind of power that raised Jesus from the dead. Think of the results of that transforming power on the forces of sin and evil in your local community. That is what revival could be.

By revival, most of us think about a series of scheduled meetings. In looking at newspaper announcements citing the scheduled meetings, one declared, REVIVAL—ONE WEEK ONLY. Another declared REVIVAL EVERY NIGHT EXCEPT SATURDAY. I would to God that these efforts of believers would result in true revival coming. Usually, our use of REVIVAL covers the work men do for Christ in the areas of church renewal and evangelism. True REVIVAL, however, is work Christ does for men.

Moving to the Northeast in 1980 brought myriad opportunities to minister to believers whose outlook is somewhat different from the prevailing views in the South. One issue was the matter of scheduling revivals. After listening to comments, I decided to change my language and talk about scheduling "revival efforts." During the series of studies in which we are engaged, perhaps we should focus on a revived church, rather than revival.

Revivals in the Word of God

When some of the children of Israel returned home from the Babylonian captivity, attention was given to the Word of God. Reading the account in the books of Ezra and Nehemiah of the spiritual awakening among God's people is thrilling. In response to the Word of God, a deep sense of conviction came upon the people. There was weeping and confessing of sins.

Upon completion of the wall on September 21, 444 BC after fifty-two days, the Jews in Jerusalem returned to the Word of God and renewed their commitment to live for the Lord. A major lesson to learn in studying the account in **Nehemiah 8-10** is that believers must confess and forsake their sins.

Nehemiah knew that national security ultimately rested, not in military might, but in spiritual integrity. The walls were not the only things in need of repair—so were the people themselves. A spiritual vacuum existed in the life of the exiles. A public assembly was called for the reading of God's Word (**Nehemiah 8:1-4**). The cry of the people showed that they were spiritually hungry (**v 1**). Entire families gathered attentively on September 27, 444 BC, just six days after the completion of the walls, for a six-hour service led by Ezra, the priest, who read and explained the Scriptures. Attentive to the Word of God, the people's hearts were turned to God and revival broke out (**8:5-18**), just as had happened in the days of Josiah and Hezekiah. Great conviction fell upon the hearts of the people. Revival fervor was characterized by worship of God (**v 6**), remorse for sin (**v 8**), joy in the Lord (**vv 10-12**), and obedience to God's Word (**vv 13-18**). There is no doubt that the same characteristics will be manifested any time in history when revival comes to the church and/or to individual Christians.

Revival brought a national attentiveness to prayer. The people prepared for prayer with public contrition (**Nehemiah 9:1-3**). The longest prayer in the Bible (**vv 4-31**) documents the people's prayer of penitence. Adoration (**vv 4-6**) was followed by a review of Israel's history, contrasting God's faithfulness with Israel's repeated failures and lapses in faith and obedience (**vv 7ff**). Turning to the present, the prayer becomes an appeal for mercy, based on God's gracious character (**v 32**). Confession of sin (**vv 33-35**) is followed by a national determination to learn from history and not repeat the failures of the past (**v 37**).

The prayer of confession (**Nehemiah 9**) is followed by an oath of allegiance; **Chapter 10** records the putting in writing of this commitment, a renewed statement of Israel's covenant obligations and the remnant's promise to fulfill it. The singers of this spiritual declaration are actually recorded (**vv 1-29**). Nehemiah, the leader, set the example (**v 1**); priests followed civil leaders (**vv 2-8**); next came heads of Levitical households (**vv 9-13**); then heads of leading lay families (**vv 14-27**); and finally the general populace (**vv 28-29**). What a day this must have been in the lives of God's people. Their commitment focused on four basic agreements: obedience to God's Word (**v 29b**); separation from mixed marriages (**v 30**); Sabbath observance (**v 31**); and support of the temple ministry (**vv 32-39**). Israel's history revealed neglect of the temple led to backsliding, so the revival made the Lord's house a priority in personal and national life, as well as stewardship of finances and temporal resources.

How long has it been since one of our services was broken up by weeping and confessing of sins? How long has it been since God took over a service? It is awfully easy to become overly familiar with the holy to the point there is no expectation for encounters with God during a service. Dr. Vance Havner observed that in many of our churches on Sunday morning, we begin at 11 o'clock sharp and end at 12 o'clock dull. Dull—apathetic—no spirit of expectation! On the other hand, we become excited in our churches over "matters of importance" that are in the long run meaningless. We engage in activities that require our time, our energy, our resources and twenty-four hours after we did them, it did not matter to anyone whether we did them or not.

Revivals in the history of the church

The book of Acts is definitive on what happens when God's people come together in one accord and in one mind seeking the Lord. Many believe that by the end of the eighth chapter of Acts as many as 100,000 to 125,000 of the 250,000 people living in the Jerusalem area were won to Christ. The Lord "added" to the church daily as folks were saved. After a while, the word "add" is no longer appropriate. The church "multiplied." One can feel the pulse of excitement that permeated the gatherings.

In **Revelation,** chapters **2** and **3**, there is a picture of the Lord Jesus Christ walking among the churches calling the people of God to repent. Those church members had lost their first love. Further, much sin had come into the church and in the lives of believers. Down through the ages, Jesus has been calling His church to repent and to return to their first love. History records periods when God's people were awakened and revived with outpourings of the Holy Spirit.

The First Awakening was among settlers in New Jersey and refugees from Moravia. It ran its course in fifty years. The Second Awakening came in 1792. Congregations were crowded, conviction was deep, and many conversions occurred. Most of the churches in New England were impacted. Great revivals swept the frontier in Kentucky and in Tennessee. The Third Awakening came in 1830. The Fourth Awakening began with a noon-day prayer meeting called by Jeremiah Lanphier in July 1857. By 1858-59, it had spread across the nation and moved into many other nations. The Fifth Awakening came in 1905.

What is revival?

Revival is an extraordinary movement of the Holy Spirit producing extraordinary results. Prior to being revived, the individual believer may have desired to do God's will, but he also desired to do his own will. He allowed the will of God to be crowded out and his own will prevailed with self on the control seat. A carnal Christian is a Christian where self is in control, not the Holy Spirit. His life is characterized by self-seeking and a careless attitude toward spiritual things.

When revived, he finds God's will central in his thinking and desires. "I've come to do Your will, O Lord." Even more glorious, he now finds himself enabled to do God's will. The God who revived Him has now enabled him.

When revival comes, there are discernible manifestations in the believer's lifestyle.

1. **Getting right with God and with others.** Confession of sins become the order of the day. Those who have sinned in private will make their confession before God whom they have wronged. Those who have sinned against others will go to these persons and make their peace. Those who have sinned publicly will find the grace of Christ to make public confession. A watching world will stand amazed as

Christians who lived like heathen now begin to manifest the love of Christ to one another. Biblical commandments and principles long trampled in the dust will be revered and restored to practice.

2. **Word of God**. Revived individuals will find themselves desiring "the sincere milk of the Word as newborn babes." They will be moved to diligent personal Bible study and to faithful application of its wonderful truths to their lives.

3. **Prayer.** Talking to God and spending time in His presence will no longer be drudgery, but pure delight. The "sweet hour of prayer" becomes a precious reality delightfully beneficiary. A revived Christian has fallen in love. The prime desire of every lover is to be with his beloved.

4. **Witnessing.** There will be a deep desire to see others saved and liberated by the power of God. There will be an agony for souls. Prayer for the eternal welfare of others will become a passion.

5. **Holiness.** Holiness will become a prime object of life. "To be like Jesus" will become the theme song of the revived. "Oh to be like Him" will be the governing desire for thought and conduct. On a daily basis, one will live the Scriptures.

6. **Fervor and excitement.** Believing that God can do for others what He has done for them, believers will march out of the revival circle as a conquering army. The result will be profound. The very revival that broke and remade the believers will pour forth upon an unsuspecting world with the same breaking and remaking power. A revival people will become instruments of revival. The recipients of grace will become the dispensers of grace. Those who neglected the Word will lead others to the Word. Those who were in need of prayer will pray for others. Those who were careless in their daily walk will stand firm as pillars of holiness raised up by God for all the world to see. Those who had been silent now become witnesses to the power of God. Wave upon wave of showers of blessings will break upon the parched earth.

The world is not going to pay much attention to all the organized efforts of the institutional church. The one thing she will pay attention to is a body of people filled with a spirit of rejoicing. When the Holy Spirit is free to operate, the inevitable result is a joy that is unspeakable and full of glory.

Revival from God

My conclusion, in studying the Word and historical accounts of spiritual awakenings, is that the breaking and remaking and the pouring forth of true revival is that God does it all. If men could produce revival, they would stand back and glory in their handiwork. But when God, who is dependent upon no man or church, does it, every single revived individual will have cause to praise Him without ceasing. Isn't this why the psalmist prayed, "Wilt Thou not revive us again, that Thy people may rejoice in Thee?" (**Psalm 85:6**).

Seeking God for revival

There are carefully laid out biblical principles covering efforts that lay the ground work for genuine revival. What comes to your mind when the word *revive* is mentioned? The term certainly suggests a return to consciousness or life. Something or someone that is revived becomes active or flourishing again. When something or someone is flourishing, there is no need for revival.

When there is only a form of godliness practiced in the church without discernable power of God present, there is a need for the church to be revived. Individuals need to be revived during seasons of moral and spiritual decline and the heart grows cold. It is when individual believers are revived that the church will be revived.

A revival is an extraordinary movement of the Holy Spirit producing extraordinary results. Revival is not the ordinary result of ordinary work. Revival is always extraordinary. As we realize that revival is truly God at work in a most unusual manner, the entire being of a believer can be stirred with longings and supplications to see just an outpouring of God's mighty power in our day.

One truth that is paramount is that God does not require gold vessels, or silver vessels in whom to do His work. He does require clean vessels. One need only read Scripture to understand the heart and readiness of God to bless His child. James admonished his readers, "Draw nigh to God, and He will draw nigh to you" (**James 4:8**). God is ready for a believer to have a closer walk with Him. One clearly sees reciprocal movement; as you draw near to God, He draws near to you. The amazing thing is that we are the ones who must take the initiative if this is ever to happen.

Seeking God for revival includes drawing near to Him. We are encouraged to come before the Throne of Grace boldly, but we are never encouraged to come thoughtlessly, or lightly, or unprepared. As surely as the priests of Moses' day needed careful preparation for divine service, so we should be careful to be certain that we come as prepared as we are bold.

Seeking God for revival encompasses the "effectual, fervent prayer [that] avails much" (**James 5:16b**). Why is this particular type of praying so rare in our day? Primarily, it is because we are not on praying ground.

When we launched the around-the-clock prayer chapel ministry in Virginia in 1978, we first needed to mobilize 168 people, each willing to pray an hour a week in the prayer chapel. This was done over a period of time. Once the prayer warriors were mobilized, a period of time was set aside to provide biblical training. This was done on Sundays prior to the evening worship service. Each week, as pastor, I prepared studies on prayer and taught them during the church training hour. Over two hundred received the training, those who had volunteered to pray an hour, those who were willing to be emergency substitutes when someone could not make his allotted hour, and some simply wanting to know more about prayer. Mimeograph stencils were prepared for duplicating the studies.

In 1980, I became president of Northeastern Bible College (NJ) and we became members of Madison Baptist Church, Madison NJ. Our pastor, in learning of the prayer chapel ministry in Virginia, asked if I would do a conference on prayer in September. My response was in the affirmative knowing that I had the materials already written that could easily be mimeographed. The materials that were developed in Virginia became the nucleus for the seventy-nine paged prayer seminar workbook, the basic teaching tool for the prayer seminars that have been conducted around the world.

Session Six, in the workbook, was entitled "Getting Ready to Prayer." The basic thesis of the study is that a believer must come to a point of conviction about any sin in his life as the starting point of getting clean before God. The content of that section was a check list of questions emanating from a list of Scriptures.

A spiritual check list

Genuine revival has always started in the hearts of God's people, one by one, as they have confessed their sins, allowing the Holy Spirit to control their lives and made themselves available for service.

Any believer who is serious about personal revival and a revived church must take time to deal with sins.

A spiritual check list developed by my friend, Jack Taylor, is provided in the **Prayer Seminar Workbook** (79 page edition). Over the years, participants in a prayer seminar have shared how helpful the Check List is in bringing into consciousness sin. A professor at the University of Pennsylvania was in a seminar. He told me that he had felt quite comfortable in his spiritual life before he used the Check List. "I thought that I was a pretty good Christian," he said, "until I completed the Check List. Now I see that I have a lot of work to do."

You will remember that David felt a deep desire to be clean before God. His prayer can be used as a model for our praying when we have the same desire. "Search me"

The will of God for every believer is that he be "Spirit-filled"—which means "Spirit-controlled." When our sins are confessed and forsaken, the Holy Spirit can take control of our lives and use us to do the will of God in daily living.

The Check List, along with directions for application, is included on pages ////. I encourage you to make a decision to use the Check List in a time of cleansing and commitment as you seek God for revival in your life and in your church. God is ready when you are. Genuine revival always starts in the hearts of God's people as they confess their sins, allow the Holy Spirit to control their lives, and make themselves available for service. A revived church will see this happen.

PREPARATION FOR PERSONAL PRAYER

There are two aspects of sin for a Christian. First, God says, "There are some things I do not want in the lives of My children." Second, God says, "There are some things that I want in the lives of all my children." What am I doing that God does not want me to do? What am I not doing that God wants me to do?

A practical suggestion is to get off by yourself with pen and paper. Ask God to show you any sins in your life. List them in order to deal with them through repentance and confession one by one. Begin by praying a prayer like David's as he sought cleansing long ago: "Search me, O God, and know my heart; try me, and know my thoughts: and see if there be any wicked way in me, and lead me in the way everlasting" (**Psalm 139:23-24**). Until you confess and forsake known sin, you cannot have a prayer life: "If I regard iniquity in my heart, the Lord will not hear me" (**Psalm 66:18**); "Behold, God's hand is not shortened that He cannot save; neither is His ear heavy that He cannot hear, but your iniquities have separated between you and your God and your sins have hid His face from you so that He cannot hear" (**Isaiah 59:1-2**).

The Word of God is a mirror

Conviction is the starting place of getting clean before God. Conviction simply means being conscious or aware of sin. Conviction is the work of the Holy Spirit (**John 16:8-11**). He uses the Word of God to bring conviction. One explanation of the lack of conviction in the lives of many Christians is that they are not in the Word of God. When a Christian is seeking God through the Word, the Holy Spirit often shows him how God sees Him.

A few years ago, my wife, Sue, and I were conducting a series of prayer seminars in several Latin American countries (Puerto Rico, Venezuela, Costa Rica, Mexico). We were having lunch in San Jose, Costa Rica. She said to me, "You have a piece of butter on your right check"—which I did not know. I said, "thank you," took my napkin, and wiped off the butter. Often, as we read His Word, the Holy Spirit says, "You've got a piece of butter on your right cheek" or WHATEVER. It is then that we can take care of the problem through repentance and confession.

The Check List

Under the leadership of the Holy Spirit, this Check List can be a tremendous help in identifying and confessing sins that often hinder genuine revival. Read the selected Scriptures that follow. Go through the questions one by one. Answer truthfully each question in the light of your life at this time. Every "yes" means a sin in your life. In reading these questions, as you are convicted of sin by the Holy Spirit, put the sin on your sin list. Once the list is completed, consider each sin one by one with a willingness to make things right. Think in terms of repenting (changing your mind) and confessing (agreeing with God, owning up to the sin and saying the same thing about it—one by one—that He says). Once you have confessed the sin, you can accept forgiveness and cleansing because that is what God will give you. "If we confess our sins, He is faithful and just to forgive us our sins, and to cleanse us from all unrighteousness" (**1 John 1:9**).

Be sure to NAME YOUR SIN to God since that is what is required by the word "confess." Be specific. For example, you might need to say, "Lord, I have not put You first in my plans" or "I have neglected Your Word and prayer." Further, do not make even the least excuse for sin of any kind in your life. Remember "he that covereth his sin shall not prosper; but whoso confesseth and forsaketh them shall have mercy" (**Proverbs 18:13**).

No matter what others do, or do not do, leave nothing undone on your part. God wants to work through you to bring about a great spiritual awakening and a revival in your church. You can begin by fulfilling, with the help of the Holy Spirit, every requirement laid out by the Lord in His Word.

1. **Matthew 6:12,14-15**. *"Forgive us our debts, as we forgive our debtors. For if ye forgive men their trespasses, your heavenly Father will also forgive you: but if ye forgive not men their trespasses, neither will your Father forgive your trespasses."*
   1) Is there anyone against whom you hold a grudge?
   2) Is there anyone whom you have not forgiven?
   3) Is there anyone you hate?
   4) Is there anyone whom you do not love?
   5) Are there any misunderstandings that you are unwilling to forgive and forget?
   6) Is there any person against whom you are harboring bitterness, resentment or jealously?
   7) Is there anyone you dislike to hear well spoken of or praised?
   8) Do you allow anything to justify a wrong attitude toward another?

2. **Matthew 6:33**. *"But seek ye first the kingdom of God and His righteousness; and all these things shall be added unto you."*
   1) Is there anything in which you have failed to put God first?
   2) Have your decisions been made after your own wisdom and desires, rather than seeking and following God's will?
   3) Do any of the following in any way interfere with your surrender and service to God: pleasures, loved ones, friendships, desires for recognition, money, your own plans?

3. **Mark 16:15**. "And He said unto them, Go ye into all the world, and preach the gospel to every creature."
   1) Have you failed to seek the lost for Christ?
   2) Have you failed to witness consistently <u>with your mouth</u> for the Lord Jesus Christ?
   3) Has your life not shown to the lost the Lord Jesus Christ?

4. **John 13:35**. *"By this shall all men know that you are My disciples, if ye have love one to another."*
   1) Are you secretly pleased over the misfortunes of another?
   2) Are you secretly annoyed over the accomplishments or advancements of another?
   3) Are you guilty of any contention or strife?
   4) Do you quarrel, argue, or engaged in "heated" discussions?
   5) Are you a partaker in any divisions, or party spirit?
   6) Are there people whom you deliberately slight?

5. **Acts 20:35**. *"It is more blessed to give than to receive."*
   1) Have you robbed God by withholding His due of time, talents, or money?
   2) Have you given less than a tenth of your income for God's work?
   3) Have you failed to support mission work either in prayer or in offering?

6. **1 Corinthians 4:2**. *"Moreover it is required in stewards, that a man be found faithful."*
   1) Are you undependable so that you cannot be trusted in the Lord's work with responsibilities?
   2) Are you allowing your emotions to be stirred for things of the Lord, then doing nothing about it?

7. **1 Corinthians 6:19-20**. *"What? Know ye not that your body is the temple of the Holy Spirit who is in you, which ye have of God, and ye are not your own? For ye are bought with a price: therefore glorify God in your body and in your spirit, which are God's."*
   1) Are you in any way careless with your body?
   2) Do you fail to care for your body as the temple of the Holy Spirit?
   3) Are you guilty of intemperance in eating and drinking?
   4) Do you have habits that are defiling your body?

8. **1 Corinthians 10:31**. *"Whether ye eat, or drink, of WHATSOEVER YE DO, do all to the glory of God."*

1) Do you take the slightest credit for anything good about you, rather than give all to the glory of God?
2) Do you talk of what you have done rather than what Christ has done?
3) Are your statements mostly about "I"?
4) Are your feelings easily hurt?
5) Have you made a pretense of being something you are not?

9. **Ephesians 3:20**. *"Now unto Him that is able to do exceedingly abundantly above all that we ask or think, according to the power that worketh in us."*
   1) Are you SELF-CONSCIOUS rather than GOD-CONSCIOUS?
   2) Do you allow feelings of inferiority to keep you from attempting things you should for God?

10. **Ephesians 4:28**. *"Let him that stole steal no more; but rather let him labour, working with his hands the thing which is good, that he may have to give to him that needeth."*
    1) Do you underpay?
    2) Do you do very little in your work?
    3) Have you been careless in the payment of your debts?
    4) Do you waste time for yourself and for others?

11. **Ephesians 4:31**. *"Let all bitterness, and wrath, and anger, and clamour, and evil speaking, be put away from you, with all malice."*
    1) Do you complain?
    2) Do you find fault?
    3) Do you have a critical attitude toward any person or thing?
    4) Are you irritable or cranky?
    5) Do you ever carry hidden anger?
    6) Do you get angry?
    7) Do you become impatient with others?
    8) Are you ever harsh or unkind?

12. **Ephesians 5:16**. *"Redeeming the time, because the days are evil."*
    1) Do you listen to unedifying radio or TV programs?
    2) Do you read unworthy magazines?
    3) Do you partake in worldly amusements?
    4) Do you find it necessary to seek satisfaction from any questionable source?
    5) Are you doing certain things that show you are not satisfied with the Lord Jesus Christ?

13. **Ephesians 5:20**. "*Giving thanks always for all things unto God and the Father, in the name of our Lord Jesus Christ.*"
    1) Have you neglected to thank Him for all things, bad and good?
    2) Have you virtually called God a liar by doubting His Word?
    3) Do you worry?
    4) Is your spiritual temperature based on your feelings instead of on the facts of God's Word?

14. **Philippians 1:21**. "*For me to live is Christ* [to live all over again], *and to die is gain.*"
    1) Are you taken up with the cares of this life?
    2) Is your conversation or heart joy over "things" rather than the Lord and His Word?
    3) Does anything mean more to you than living for and pleasing Christ?

15. **Philippians 2:14**. "*Do all things without murmurings and disputings.*"
    1) Do you ever by word or deed seek to hurt someone?
    2) Do you gossip?
    3) Do you speak unkindly concerning people when they are not present?
    4) Do you carry prejudice against true Christians because they are of some different group than yours, or because they do not see everything exactly like you?

16. **Philippians 4:4**. "*Rejoice in the Lord always: and again I say, Rejoice.*"
    1) Have you neglected to seek to be pleasing to Him in all things?
    2) Do you carry any bitterness toward God?
    3) Have you complained against Him in any way?
    4) Have you been dissatisfied with His provision for you?
    5) Do you have any reservations as to what you would or would not do concerning anything that might be His will?
    6) Have you disobeyed some direct leading from Him?

17. **Colossians 3:9**. "*Lie not one to another, seeing that ye have put off the old man with his deeds.*"
    1) Do you engage in empty and unprofitable conversation?
    2) Do you ever lie?
    3) Do you ever exaggerate?
    4) Do you ever cheat?

    5)   Do you ever steal?

    6)   Carefully consider: Do you overcharge?

18. **2 Timothy 2:22**. *"Flee also youthful lusts: but follow righteousness, faith, charity, peace, with them that call on the Lord out of a pure heart."*
1) Do you have personal habits that are not pure?
2) Do you allow impure thoughts about the opposite sex to stay in your mind?
3) Do you read that which is impure or suggests unholy thoughts?
4) Do you indulge in any unclean entertainment?
5) Are you guilty of the lustful look?

19. **Hebrews 10:25**. *"Not forsaking the assembling of ourselves together, as the manner of some is; but exhorting one another; and much more, as ye see the day approaching."*
1) Do you stay away from meetings of preaching the gospel?
2) Do you whisper or think about other things while God's Word is being read or preached?
3) Are you irregular in attendance at services?
4) Do you neglect to attend and to participate in prayer meetings?
5) Have you neglected/slighted daily private prayer?
6) Have you neglected thanksgiving at meals?
7) Have you neglected family devotions?

20. **Hebrews 13:7**. *"Remember them which have the rule over you, who have spoken unto you the Word of God: whose faith follow, considering the end of their conversation."*
1) Do you hesitate to submit to leaders in the church or elsewhere?
2) Are you lazy?
3) Do you rebel at requests given to you to help in the work of the gospel?
4) Do you have in any way a stubborn or unteachable spirit?

21. **James 1:27**. *"Pure religion and undefiled before God and the Father is this, To visit the fatherless and widows in their affliction and to keep himself unspotted from the world."*
1) Have you allowed yourself to become "spotted" by the world?
2) Is your manner of dress pleasing to God?
3) Do you spend beyond what is pleasing to God on anything?
4) Do you neglect to pray about the things you buy?

22. **James 4:6**. "*But He giveth more grace, Wherefore He saith, God resisteth the proud, but giveth more grace unto the humble.*"
   1) Do you feel that you have done quite well as a Christian?
   2) Do you feel that you are not so bad?
   3) Do you feel that you are good enough?
   4) Are you stubborn?
   5) Do you insist on having your own way?
   6) Do you insist on your own "rights"?

23. **James 3:11**. "*Doth a fountain send forth at the same place sweet water and bitter?*"
   1) Have you dishonored Him and hindered His work by criticizing His servants?
   2) Have you failed to pray regularly for your pastor and other spiritual leaders?
   3) Do you find it hard to be corrected?
   4) Is there rebellion toward one who wants to restore you?
   5) Are you more concerned about what people will think than what will be pleasing to God?

Conclusion

When you have been honest and truthful in the matter of admitting your sins (commission and omission) and have repented (changed your mind), then you are ready for cleansing. Sins that are admitted are sins that are confessed. "*Who can understand his errors? Cleanse Thou me from secret faults*" (**Psalm 19:12**).

Remember three things: (1) When the sin is against God, confess it to God, and make things right with God; (2) When the sin is against another person, confess it to God, and make things right with the other one; and (3) When the sin is against a group (including the church), confess it to God, and make it right with the group (church).

When there is FULL CONFESSION, there will be FULL CLEANSING. Then the joy of the Lord will follow. Then there can be testimony and prayer in the power of the Holy Spirit. The Check List will help Christians obey the command in **Ephesians 5:18**: BE SPIRIT-FILLED, which literally means SPIRIT-CONTROLLED. When our known sins are confessed [agreed to] and forsaken, the Holy Spirit can control our lives and use us to touch lives for the Lord Jesus Christ.

Study Sixteen

In a psalm attributed to the sons of Korah, a prayer was made that expresses a desire of many believers today: "Will you not revive us again, That Your people may rejoice in You?" (**Psalm 85:6**). During this series of study, attention is given to a praying church. After all, the only thing that the Lord Jesus Christ left behind when He finished His work on earth and returned to Heaven was a praying church.

America, a nation in trouble, needs a revived church. There was a time when Christianity shaped the social, political, moral, religious, and intellectual landscape of these United States. Gradually, little by little and step by step, we have come loose from the anchors that have steadied us. The result is the breakdown of marriage and family, a rise in crime and violence, and a callous disregard for life. To use more precise terms, these days are characterized by relativism (the denial of absolute meaning) and narcissism (worship of self).

Christianity is under attack. We need to discern what is happening in our nation and not be ignorant of Satan's devices. We need to know the provisions God has made for His children and His church. We need to understand that prayer is the work that must come before all other work (**John 14:12-14**).

No person in my memory has grasped the truth of a praying church more than my friend who is now with the Lord, Armin Gesswein. These studies are for anyone who cares about the church.

PRAYER—WHERE THE ACTION IS
By Armin Gesswein

A veil must be removed from our eyes if we are to look into the heart of prayer. The Bible does this for us. It shows us that prayer is the action, not only of man but of the living God Himself. It is one of the ways He expresses His infinity finitely. *"Let us therefore come boldly unto the throne of grace, that we may obtain mercy, and find grace to help in time of need"* (**Hebrews 4:16**). G. Campbell Morgan said that the "time of need" means "the nick of time."

"Whenever God is about to do any kind of work, He always begins with prayer."

111

Let us get right to the point. Whenever God is about to do any kind of work He always begins with prayer. In God's plan for man, prayer is not everything, but everything is accomplished by prayer.

This is an age of science and of very exciting discoveries. But by far the most fascinating field for discovery and wonder is the field of prayer. When we consider what Jesus Christ has promised to those who know how to pray, I wonder if we have more than scratched the surface of this subject.

For example, the Lord promises *"If ye ask anything in My name, I will do it." "All things, whatsoever ye shall ask in prayer, believing, ye shall receive." "What things soever ye desire, when ye pray, believe that ye receive them, and ye shall have them."* As if that were not enough, He promises: *"If ye abide in Me, and My words abide in you, ye shall ask what ye will, and it shall be done unto you."*

With promises like these—more bona fide than blue-ribbon stocks—one would think that people everywhere would get excited about prayer and meetings for prayer would be crowded, with standing or kneeling room only. In view of His offers, our weak little prayer meetings must be a sad sight to God!

God's entire plan for man is a prayer plan. There is nothing like it in all the universe. As I sit writing this, Jesus Christ our risen and ascended Lord is "up there" seated on the throne at the right hand of God the Father. In plain language the Bible says, *"He ever liveth to make intercession for* [us]." He is our high priest *"forever after the order of Melchisdec."*

This really means that the whole redemptive work of Christ has now passed into prayer. Who of us can comprehend it all? Our Christ is a praying Christ. Prayer has priority with Him, and if I am to live like Christ I must pray.

There is almost nothing to compare with the expanse of prayer. Prayer is cosmic. I believe that if our eyes could be opened—if this veil of sense and space and time could suddenly be removed so that we could look in there where God works, we would see the whole universe is shot through and through with prayer action. We would see the throne of God is the busiest place in all the cosmos.

We would see how everything is related to prayer. We would also see the angels of God ascending and descending, myriads of them, all over the earth. We would see millions of prayers going up and answers coming down. The man whom God most uses in a given time is the man who gets the prayers of God's people. This was the secret behind the ministry of the late

Charles E. Fuller. Many recall how he used to ask for people to pray during his broadcast.

Again, if we could see the inner action of God behind the veil, we would also see that God is only a prayer away from any one of us. We would see, too, how disposed God is to answer. We would never doubt nor fear nor give up. God has, so to speak, wired the whole universe for prayer.

He is only a prayer away from your burden now. He is only a prayer away from your longing, your sign, your tear, your problem, the heartache you have for your children. He is only a prayer away from your shaky married life. He is only a prayer away from the inward rebellion that is trying to break up your life. "*Whosoever shall call on the name of the Lord shall be saved* [delivered]." Why not call upon Him?

"All the great people of the Bible were praying people."

We have already spoken of the veil that must be removed if we are to see God in action. And this is where the Bible comes in; it is a revelation, an unveiling. From Genesis to Revelation, the Scriptures unveil the wonderful prayer action of God. **All the great people of the Bible were praying people**. They have many secrets, but this is their greatest.

What mighty answers the Bible unveils! Abraham prayed and became the father of a new nation. Jacob wrestled with God in prayer and his name was changed to Israel. Moses prayed and saved a nation. Samuel prayer and turned a whole nation back to God. Elijah prayed and withstood all the massive idolatry of his day. Daniel prayed and became the power behind the world powers of his day, Babylon and Media-Persia. Time fails to tell of other prophets of God.

The veil is lifted ever more fully and we are allowed to see the prayer life of Jesus Christ Himself. In Him, we behold the complete prayer life, the greatest ever displayed on earth. No wonder Dr. James Stewart, of Scotland, wrote: "The praying Christ is the supreme argument for prayer."

As we see Christ, we discover new things. One is this: in His life EVERYTHING was done by prayer and in effect He turns to us and says: "This is the prayer life I want you to have. I brought it down here and lived it out for you. My plan is now to dwell in you. You will now be able to pray in My name. I shall live and prayer in you; and you will get My kind of answers.

Most Christians do not know how rich they are: "*Christ in you, the hope of glory*!" As Christians we have this new and different prayer life: Christ living in us. We ought to excel in prayer.

Prayer alone is not a Christian distinctive. People all over the world pray because man was made for prayer. Everywhere we find temples, shrines, altars. But the Christian prayer life is different. It is characterized by the praying of Christ. That is the Christian distinctive. We are now to share His kind of praying and His kind of answers.

As we go through the Bible the veil is constantly lifted from our eyes, revealing Christ's prayer plan for man. The Book of the Revelation is God's final unveiling—the Apocalypse. Now we are allowed to see right into heaven itself, into the very throne of God. Before this we saw the action of that throne; now we see the throne itself. Forty times in this book, the spotlight is on God's throne.

God's throne—that is where the action is! The events that shape history, the destiny of the nations and the happenings in nature are governed at that throne. The astronauts' landing on the moon is nothing compared to the ascension of Jesus Christ and His landing at the very throne of God—crowned as "*King of kings, and Lord of lords . . . head over all things to the church, which is His body, the fullness of Him that filleth all in all.*"

An old philosopher said, "Give me a place to stand and I will move the earth." Jesus Christ has found that place. And He is moving the earth from the vantage point of His throne.

"*Behold, a throne was set in heaven, and One sat on the throne . . . I beheld, and I heard the voice of many angels round about the throne and the beasts and the elders: and the number of them was ten thousand times ten thousand and thousands of thousands . . . Worthy is the Lamb that was slain to receive power, and riches, and wisdom, and strength, and honour, and glory, and blessing.*" Such are the scenes in the Revelation. It unveils the very throne room.

More, the Apocalypse really opens up the secret of the whole universe. Three lessons stand out to me.

1. Prayer is CELESTIAL. It not only is for us down here, but it is most mighty and continuous up there.
2. Prayer is COSMIC. Of this I have already spoken.
3. Prayer is CENTRAL. As a vast telephone communication system goes through a central control, so prayer is centered at Christ's throne, the center of all things created. Everything is under His control. By prayer we can talk directly with the King of kings and Lord of lords, the Almighty Ruler of the whole universe.

Prayer—always a person-to-person call

But prayer is not just a number we dial. It is always a person-to-person call. We are temples made for prayer and made for God. As we can reach people around the world by telephone, so by prayer, through Christ's central throne room, we can touch the need of our missionaries right now, as well as the neighbor next door.

No one suddenly gets chummy with God out in the Elysian fields or in the Milky Way. We must go to the throne to find God. One day in Chicago I said to a friend, "We are going across the hall to talk to that lawyer about Christ, but we can reach him only by first talking to Christ. We must pray. Christ must reach and win him." Not only is that the quickest ay, it is the only way in winning men and women to Christ.

A praying church

One question remains: How does all this relate to the church? What connection does Christ's throne have with your local congregation? Jesus said, *"Upon this rock I will build My church; and the gates of hell shall not prevail against it"* (**Matthew 16:18**). These words are forever settled in heaven. They are not negotiable at some summit conference. Christ will write the last chapter of history.

Now the question arises: How would Jesus go about building a church like that? For He is designer, architect and builder. How would He construct this most powerful force ever to be put together on this earth? This it would have to be if the "gates of hell" were not to prevail against it.

I can picture Him saying something like this: "What form shall I give to My church? How shall I construct it? When I was down there on earth I did everything by prayer, and I'm still doing everything by prayer up here on My throne. This I will do: I will build My church as a praying congregation—every member of it. Down there it will be a praying church; up here I am the praying Christ. In this way I will have perfect contact, perfect connection and perfect communication with My church at all times and in all places on earth."

This is exactly what we see when we open the Book of Acts. It has been called the "book of the church." A shaper focus suggests that is the book of the praying church. Every member was a praying member. *"These all continued with one accord in*

115

prayer and supplication, with the women, and Mary, the mother of Jesus, and with His brethren" (**Acts 1:14**).

Once more in this book, the veil is lifted from our eyes. Here we see Christ performing His highest miracle on earth before He went to heaven. The more we contemplate it, the more wonderful the miracle of that prayer meeting appears to be. Out of it comes all the exciting developments that make up these "Acts."

In Jesus' life—everything done by prayer

Every single member of the church was at the prayer meeting. What a miracle! Nothing kept anyone home. No sickness, no headache, no heartache, no accident, no funeral, no games, no sporting event, no schoolwork or homework. No weather conditions, no social event, no banquet, no family cares, no visiting relatives. No Jewish cares connected with the coming great feast of Pentecost. No business deals. No buying or selling on the part of the Jews (the world's greatest sellers). None of these kept anyone away from the first Upper Room prayer meeting.

How do you feel about the prayer meeting? You say: "Well, I wouldn't want to belong to a church that doesn't have one, but I don't especially want to go." This kind of slack rope must be taken up if we are to see true revival in our congregations.

If you were to ask me what is the greatest discovery I have made concerning the church. I would have to say it was the day I discovered in Scripture that when Christ built the church He built a praying church. And if you then would ask me what is the greatest decision I have made in the light of that discovery, I would have to say it was the day I decided to go to prayer meetings. I was a minister before I ever did this, or ever knew anything about a prayer meeting. Now, by God's grace, I want to be involved also in this form of praying all of my life.

As it was in the beginning, so it will be again. The world has yet to see what God can, and will, do through a whole congregation dedicated to Him in prayer.

Study Seventeen

Are you ready to plead with God for genuine revival in your life, in your church and across the nation? If so, you yourself must be on praying ground. Intercessory praying is simply coming to the Father, through the Son, in the power of the Holy Spirit on behalf of others. An intercessor is a go-between, literally standing between God and some person or circumstance. It is impossible to do the work of intercession when there are unconfessed and unforsaken sins in your life.

When you become serious about praying for revival in your church, be sensitive to the Holy Spirit's promptings. He will bring to your mind things that you are doing that God does not want His children to do and will let you see things that you are not doing that God wants you to do. When you become aware that there is a specific sin in your life (either omission or commission), that is biblical conviction. Once you are aware of sin, you must repent, which means to change you mind about that sin. You must confess specifically each sin. When you do, there will be forgiveness and cleansing (**1 John 1:9**). Your direction will change. Then you must surrender to the Holy Spirit. You will then be on praying ground and ready to seek God for revival in your life and in your church.

The sense of praying for revival is to ask God's hand to move—to ask God to do something. Jesus gave intercessory prayer principles in His story about the man who went to a friend at midnight asking, on behalf of one in need, for three loaves of bread: (1) Shamelessly knocking. You do not have to apologize to God when you come as an intercessor. You are not going to a stranger, you are going to your Father, "Abba, Father." We, too, need to come boldly to the Throne of Grace when we need to find mercy and help in time of need (**Hebrews 4:16**). (2) Be specific. If you were my neighbor and asked if I needed you to bring me something from the grocery store, I could not simply ask you to bring me some "food," You would have to ask me to be specific. What is that you want God to do? Be specific. (3) Persistence. The man arose, opened the door, and gave the seeker three loaves of bread for one reason, persistence. The fellow kept on knocking.

What is it that you want God to do in your life and in the life of your church? The following are examples of specific requests that can be prayed for yourself and the believers in your church to use as you seek God for revival. Since revival comes from God, it is important that we confess to Him that we desire Him to send revival.

Specific requests

1. A spirit of humility and brokenness. "Father, grant a spirit of brokenness and repentance to the believers of _____ Church (**Isaiah 57:15; James 4:6**).

2. A deeper love for the Lord Jesus Christ. "Father, enable the believers of _____ Church to return to You as our first love" (**Revelation 2:4; 1 John 4:1-3**).

3. A deeper understanding and awareness of His holiness. "Father, give the believers of _____Church a fresh and powerful vision of Your holiness (**Isaiah 6:1-5; 1 Peter 1:15-16**).

4. A hunger for the Word of God and a readiness to obey its teachings. "Father, cause the believers of _____ Church to be receptive to, and responsive to, Your Word (**Psalm 119:97, 103; 1 John 2:3-6**). "Father, cause the believers of _____Church to become contrite (broken) and tremble at Your Word" (**Isaiah 66:2b**).

5. An agonizing burden for lost people and an unceasing desire to share the Gospel with them. "Father, cause your people at _____ Church to become burdened for the unsaved and to go weeping to them with God's Word (**Psalm 126:5-6; Matthew 18:18-20; 2 Corinthians 5:10; Romans 9:1-3**).

Remember to start with yourself. Ask God to do the things in your life that you are asking for others. As we continue the studies on a praying church and a revived church, other examples of specific requests will be given. Don't be surprised if the Holy Spirit gives you additional insights as you begin to bring these specific requests to the Lord. He will likely give you more Scriptures to use as you pray for revival.

Vance Havner

During my time serving as a pastor, I was often challenged by messages from Vance Havner. The Lord used his words to stir my heart to self-examination. One message that pointed out how far the church has drifted was entitled "If THIS were "THAT." Since it is important for us to come to the point that we understand what has happened to the church, and to the believers that constitute a church, I want to share the message with you. "Father, revived the believers of _____ Church so

118

that we may rejoice in You (**Psalm 85:6**)." "Restore, dear Father, the believers of _____ Church; make Your face to shine on us that we may be delivered from our drifting away from you and from our backsliding nature" (**Psalm 80:7**).

If THIS were "THAT"
by Vance Havner

On the day of Pentecost, when the multitude saw the early church filled with the Spirit, they asked, "What does this mean?" Peter replied, *"This is that which was spoken by the prophet Joel"* (**Acts 2:16**). _After his sermon the listeners asked, "What shall we do?"

We have tried to reverse that order today. We expect men to ask, "What shall we do?" before they have seen enough of the power of God in action to make them ask, "What does this mean?" In our desperation, we have staged religious extravaganzas, stirred up religious excitements and simulated religious ecstasies, but the multitude is not crying, "What shall we do?"

In this day when "Amazing Grace" has become a best seller, when Gospel rock packs auditoriums, when the name of Jesus is at an all-time high of popularity in fads today that fade tomorrow—in such a time there comes from many directions the question, "Is this revival? Is this an outpouring of the Holy Spirit? *Is THIS 'THAT'*?"

The question is its own answer. The very fact that we ask it implies doubt and uncertainty. If genuine revival ever comes, we will know it! A true work of God is always self-authenticating. It bears its own credentials and needs no conference of experts to identify it.

If this were "that," if we were having an authentic spiritual awakening, there would be a return to the authority of the Bible, the inerrant inspiration of the Word of God. Some of the brethren battling for orthodoxy might well major on calling the Church to repentance, for when the Church repents, she forsakes her doubt, and liberalism does not have a leg to stand on. What argument could never accomplish comes naturally (supernaturally) when men turn to God.

If this were "that," our orthodox churches would experience needed revival. It is possible to be as straight as a gun barrel theologically and as empty as a gun barrel spiritually. Francis Schaeffer has pointed out that the great moments in church

119

history have come when there has been a return to pure doctrine, along with a fresh experience of the Holy Spirit.

One writer who has spent his life in the separatist movement expresses grief that the stress on purity of doctrine has not been accompanied by an emphasis on true revival. The result of all this has been a cold fundamentalism, and nothing is deader than dead orthodoxy. The Pharisees belonged in that category, and they drew the severest condemnation ever uttered by our Lord.

If this were "that," there would be profound conviction of sin, confession and forsaking of sin. Sin would not be airily dismissed as immaturity, arrested development and biological growing pains. Parents no longer think their unsaved children are lost. Whatever happened to that old word, it still designates the kind of people Christ came to seek and to save. Johnny may be a good boy, but so was the rich young ruler! Old-fashioned sinners are harder to find these days than whooping cranes.

Prodigals are not returning home confessing, "I have sinned." They are being rehabilitated by social action programs in modernized hogpens out in the far country. We cannot expect God to take away our sins by forgiving them if we will not put them away than forsaking them.

If we were having revival, *If this were "that,"* the divorce rate would drop, houses would become homes and marriages would be for life. It would not be fashionable for unwed college students to live like man and wife in dormitories. Pornography, nudity, homosexuality, and other abominations would not be accepted. The husband would be the head and the wife the heart of the home. Motherhood would be elevated again to its true importance in spite of Women's Lib. Discipline would be restored in home and church, from which it has disappeared almost entirely.

If this were "that," it would make its impact on lawlessness and crime. It is as though all highway signs were torn down and all motorists left free to follow their own judgment. There is no king in Israel and every man does what is right in his own eyes. A genuine visitation of God would do more for law and order than politicians running for office ever promised in their wildest oratory.

If this were "that," there would be reconciliation and restitution among Christians. Before we offer our gifts at the altar, we would get right with the offending or offended brother. The church is rent today with all the sins Paul enumerated: envy, strife, divisions, swellings, tumults, schisms, variance, debates, contentions. One might add tattling, gossip, backbiting, jealousy among the flock—and sometimes among the preachers! Husbands and wives, parents and children, neighbors—all would be reconciled.

Personality clashes in church staffs would disappear. Sins of tongue and temper, and all the evils that beset Corinth long ago and plague us today, would be dealt with. Zacchaeus would straighten out his crooked business practices.

Two-faced hypocrites who still steal widows' houses and for a pretense make long prayers, would get right with God and man. Only a mighty moving of the Spirit can clear the scandal and strife in the Church today so that we cleanse ourselves from all filthiness of flesh and spirit, perfecting holiness in the fear of God.

If this were "that," there would be a decline of worldliness in the Church. Worldliness is an extinct work in our preaching today. Secularism has taken its place, and since few people know what secularism means, it does not endanger the preacher's popularity. We used to call on Christians to come out and be separate. Today, even among conservatives, the trend is to get "in" and get with it. Anything that even sounds like separation from the world is abhorred as though it were the bubonic plague.

The world and the professing Church first flirted with each other, then fell in love, and now the wedding is upon us.

If we had revival, Christians would learn afresh that the friend of the world is the enemy of God. There would be an outbreak of the original New Testament Christianity.

If this were "that," we would be delivered from such popular aberrations as the notion that we must dress like the world, talk like the world, sing like the world in order to reach it for Christ. One does not have to look like a clown in order to witness in a circus. I used to preach quite often in a rescue mission. I did not find it necessary to dress like a bum to make my ministry effective.

If this were "that," there would be a recovery of modesty in dress and deportment. Christians would be different in appearance, and would set a standard for a sex-crazy generation. What matters most is the heart, but the world cannot see our hearts, it sees our clothes and judges accordingly.

If this were "that," the sanctity of the Lord's Day would be restored. What used to be the Lord's Day is now lost in the weekend. In the new calendar of long holidays and four-day work weeks, God's old arrangement of work and rest is a thing of the past.

My own denomination, Southern Baptist, says in its statement of faith that on the Lord's Day we should "refrain from secular employments, works of necessity and works of mercy excepted." Sunday football would hardly qualify as an exception, yet it is accepted both by Christian players and by spectators, including the multitude that no man can number viewing sports by television on Sunday afternoon.

The church began to degenerate, as Augustine tells us, when holy days were merged with holidays to please the influx of new pagan members. Today we have moved from the catacombs to the colosseum and revised our standards to suit a generation of pleasure-lovers who do not love God.

If this were "that," there would be a mighty impact on evil institutions and a powerful surge of social righteousness. There was a day when preachers fought the liquor traffic. They did not believe in mopping up the floor while we left the faucet running!

Today even religious leaders have a good word for cocktails, and Paul's advice to Timothy about a little wine for his stomach's sake is one of the most overworked verses I can think of. There must be an epidemic of stomach trouble among church members today! This smiling tolerance from the pulpit is a concession to the potential alcoholics of the country club.

We are hearing that the New Testament does not teach total abstinence. The only reason given for teetotalism is that we should not drink if it causes the weaker brother to stumble. That is one reason, but it is not the main one. I do not need a Bible verse to justify leaving liquor alone. Plain common sense should keep anybody from touching anything so dangerous to body, mind, family and other people.

A real revival would take bars out of homes, put Bibles where beer has been, giving men and women a new stimulant from Heaven without a hangover when they are no longer drunk with wine, but filled with the Spirit.

In the text quoted by Peter from Joel, the ministers are called upon to weep because a pagan world taunts a powerless people of God. When we meet God's conditions, then the Spirit will be poured out.

This is not to say that the Spirit is not working today. The Spirit is at work in faithful Christians, Bible preachers, New Testament churches and a multitude of young people. But there is no mighty awakening producing such evidences of revival as we have been enumerating.

There is also the danger of false revival, worse than no revival at all. Satan is the Great Imitator. When Moses produced his miracles, Jannes and Jambres were on hand with their counterfeits. Satan mixes tares with the wheat. He works disguised as an angel of light. He creates a wave of simulated religion that would deceive if possible the very elect. Even good people are confused and afraid to oppose these false movements lest they fight against God. The sin against the Holy Spirit lay in ascribing the work of God to the devil. We may see the reverse order today in the work of the Devil being ascribed to God.

If revival comes, it will be in the providence of God, and in His time. We cannot regulate the Holy Spirit like clockwork. One thing is certain: There will be no revival until the Church repents. Our Lord's last word to the Church was "Repent," and His last word to the Church is the last work in the Church today.

If this were "that," it would produce the results we have indicated. These revival conditions cannot be corrected merely by denunciation from the pulpit. They can be exposed by such preaching, and they should be. Such preaching brings conviction, but these evils can be corrected only by conversion and the continuing work of the Holy Spirit within.

When such revival comes, there will be evidence, fruits meet for repentance, not visible generally today.

When such revival comes, we shall know it.

Conclusion

A good exercise would be to study Dr. Havner's message line by line and make a list of matters that obviously need to be corrected. Beginning with yourself, deal with any issues that are keeping you from having full fellowship with the Lord. Then, begin to pray that members of your own church would become conscious of any sins in their lives that are reflected in the message. God is waiting and ready to hear our prayers and heal our land.

I encourage you, also, to pray for your pastor. Revival usually comes when God gives His people bold, faithful, and fearless preachers of the Word of God. True and powerful preaching brings conviction of sin and is used by God to revive His people. Pray that your pastor will preach the Word of God with power, conviction, and authority (**1 Corinthians 2:1-4; 2 Timothy 3:16-4:4**).

Study Eighteen

As we have watched things unfold, we have felt in our souls that we must have revival. That this world needs a revival of Christianity is not the question of the hour. The burning question for us all to consider is: "What will happen to civilization within the next decade if we do not have a genuine spiritual awakening?" This question not only involves preachers and churches; it is the major question that confronts every official in the United States from President Bush down to every leader and decision-maker in our government, every leader in our armed forces, every business executive, every labor leader, every home and individual in the whole world without regard to race or creed. Frankly, we have reached a crisis point.

What the Bible says

As never before, it is important for us to keep things in a biblical perspective. As I have prayed for America, the Holy Spirit has continued to call me back to the Word of God. What does the Word of God say? What light does the Scripture shed on our human predicament? My commitment to the readers of **Doorkeeper Waymarks** is to seek God's message from the Bible and then share what He has put on my heart. I believe that God has a Word for His church that has been set forth already in the Bible. It may not be the word that we want, but it needs to be set before us anyway. Jesus said, "You shall know the truth and the truth shall make you free" (**John 8:32**)—provided that we bring our lives and thoughts into conformity and harmony with that truth.

You will remember that King Zedekiah, the last king of Judah, during very desperate times brought Jeremiah out of the prison into a private room and implored Jeremiah: "Is there any Word from the Lord?" (**Jeremiah 37:17**). There was a word, but it was not one that comforted King Zedekiah.

It is unbelievable that many in the church, who are numbered among the believers, no longer accept the authority of the Bible. Nevertheless, the Bible remains true. When the Bible says it, that settles it, whether any one of us believes it or not. Secular humanism has beguiled many in the present generation into thinking that there are no absolute truths, that truth is always relative. Untrue! What insights do the Scriptures provide to guide us in these troubled times? The world is heading for a final battle between the God and the forces of evil. Many Christians, however, are ignorant of the Word of God because they have turned to human wisdom and the traditions of men (**Mark 7:13**). Churches are full of people who are ignorant of what God has revealed about things to come.

The Day of the Lord

On the home front, the forces of evil are moving forward with openness and seeming confidence that their views will prevail in America. In earlier years of my fifty-one year ministry, the devil's approaches were subtle. Now they are brazenly open. What my friend, Dr. Henry Morris, has termed **The Long War Against God** seems to be coming to a climax. Look at the lifestyles that prevail in America. It's really amazing how materialistic that we have become as God has poured out His bountiful blessings upon our nation. Our obsession with larger houses, bigger screen TVs, sportier cars, the latest gadgets, and faster boats is truly something to behold, especially, when one morning we're going to wake up, everything we have is gone up in smoke. That is going to happen!

That's the point Peter wanted to make in his epistle. He wants us to know that when "the day of the Lord will come as a thief in the night, in which the heavens will pass away with a great noise, and the [very] elements will melt with fervent heat; both the earth and the works that are in will be burned up" (**2 Peter 3:10**). Those material things that we have come to love so much will all be gone. Of course, once we understand this, Peter wants us to act appropriately. "Therefore, since all these things will be dissolved, what manner of persons ought you to be in holy conduct and godliness, looking for and hastening the coming of the day of God, because of which the heavens will be dissolved being on fire, and the elements will melt with fervent heat (**vv 11-12**)?" He asks: "What kind of people ought we to be?" And he answers, "you ought to live holy and godly lives" as you "look forward to a new heaven and a new earth, the home of righteousness (**v 13**)." A holy and godly life, marked by growth in the grace and knowledge of the Lord Jesus Christ is what is needed in our day.

On the international front, the forces of evil are moving forward with openness and seeming confidence that their views will prevail in the world. The problem of the Middle East can only be properly understood in theological terms. Israel lies at the very heart of a violent confrontation between the spiritual

126

powers of Islam and the Word of God (**Daniel 10:13, Ephesians 6:12**). Islam is confident that it has the final revelation of the Word of God and that it represents the fulfillment of the work of God among the nations of the world.

During the past few months, my study has centered on a revived church in our day. There have been spiritual awakenings that have been documented and I have read the accounts with great interest.

Every true Christian knows that there are a few fundamental things that must take place before a revival will be sent from God. In the last study, attention was given to confessing and forsaking known sin. As long as there is sin in the lives of God's children, there is sin in the church. Sin in the church blocks revival and hampers soul-winning efforts. The Word of God is plain to the individual Christian: "[When] I regard iniquity in my heart, the Lord won't hear" (**Psalm 66:18**). The Word of God is plain to the church: "Behold, the Lord's hand is not shortened, that it cannot save; nor His ear heavy, that it cannot hear. But your iniquities have separated you from your God; and your sins have hid His face from you, so that He will not hear" (**Isaiah 59:1-2**). When there is known and unconfessed sin, God will neither hear nor answer prayers.

Sin in the camp

The picture drawn in an incident at Ai, as the children of Israel moved into the Promised Land is haunting, indeed. After the destruction of Jericho is recounted, a striking statement is given: "So the Lord was with Joshua, and his fame spread throughout all the country" (**Joshua 6:27**). God had promised Israel a land flowing with milk and honey as their inheritance. After wandering in the wilderness for forty years, it was time for them to enter in to claim His promises. The account of their defeat at Ai is given. The word had been that Israel need not send a large contingency into battle, "Do not weary all the people there, for the people of Ai are few" (**7:3**). Consequently, about three thousand men went up. Amazingly enough, they were routed by the men of Ai: "And the men of Ai struck down about thirty-six men, for they chased them from before the gate as far as Shebarim, and struck them down on the descent; therefore the hearts of the people [of Israel] melted like water" (**7:5**).

One thing that Joshua had learned serving as Moses' second-in-command was what to do when trouble comes; take your burdens to the Lord in prayer. That is exactly what he did: "Then

Joshua tore his clothes, and fell to the earth on his face before the ark of the Lord until evening, both he and the elders of Israel; and they put dust on their heads. And Joshua said, 'Alas, Lord God, why have You brought this people over the Jordan at all—to deliver us into the hand of the Amorites, to destroy us? Oh, that we had been content, and dwelt on the other side of the Jordan" O Lord, what shall I say when Israel turns its back before its enemies? For the Canaanites and all the inhabitants of the land will hear of it, and surround us, and cut off our name from the earth. Then what will You do for Your great name?'" (**7:6-9**).

God heard the cry of Joshua and His answer was blunt and direct. "So the Lord said to Joshua: 'Get up! Why do you lie thus on your face? Israel has sinned, and they have also transgressed My covenant which I commanded them. For they have even taken some of the accursed things, and have both stolen and deceived; and they have also put it among their own stuff. Therefore the children of Israel could not stand before their enemies, but turned their backs before their enemies, because they have been doomed to destruction. Neither will I be with you any more, unless you destroy accursed from among you. Get up, sanctify yourselves for tomorrow, because thus says the Lord God of Israel: There is an accursed thing in your midst, O Israel; you cannot stand before your enemies until you take away the accursed thing from among you'" (**7:10-13**). There was sin in the camp that had to be dwelt with before God's hand of blessing rested upon His children.

Every true Christian knows that before a revival will be sent by God, there must be prayer. It is common knowledge to every follower of Christ that no one need expect a revival to come to the people of God until we pray. That fact needs no debating. "If My people who are called by My name will humble themselves and pray and seek My face and turn from their wicked ways, then will I hear from Heaven, and will forgive their sin and heal their land" (**2 Chronicles 7:14**). Then, why wait? Why not pray?

No substitute for prayer

There are some very good reasons why we are not praying more for revival. We find them clearly revealed in **Genesis 32** in the story of Jacob when he was compelled to face his adversary, his own brother, Esau, who had murder in his heart. First, Jacob tried to substitute knowledge for prayer. He was far smarter than his brother and out-smarted every person with whom he dealt. He was the shrewdest Jew in history, but his vast store of

128

knowledge and success was no substitute for prayer. Second, he tried to substitute riches for prayer. He sent alluring gifts to his brother. Never were our churches, our institutions, and our boards so prosperous. But money is no substitute for prayer. Third, Jacob tried to substitute organization for prayer. As you read the story, you will find that Jacob divided his people who were traveling with him and the herds and flocks and camels into two bands in order to escape Esau. But his organization failed. We are super-organizers today in our religious activities as well as in secular life. But organization, good as it is, is no substitute for prayer. Fourth, he tried to substitute numbers for prayer. He could have sent his gifts to Esau by the hand of one or two men, but he sent numbers to make a great display of might. In this, he sadly failed for Esau had numbers, too. He had 400 armed men with him. The devil has more people here on earth than God has. Numbers are no substitute for prayer. Fifth, he tried to substitute a program for prayer. He had concocted the best variety of maneuverings to be found in any such store in the Bible. The were well planned programs and skillfull carried out, but they did not work. We have plans, methods, and programs, which we believer are of necessity and are God given, but they are no substitute for prayer.

God our only help

Finally, Jacob came to the end of the row. His arm of flesh had failed him. He had but one alternative if he would escape death at the hands of Esau. That alternative was to pray to God for divine help, "Then Jacob said, 'O God of my father Abraham and God of my father Isaac, the Lord who said to me, "Return to your country and to your kindred, and I will deal well with you"; I am not worthy of the least of all the mercies and of all the truth which You have shown Your servant; for I crossed over this Jordan with my staff, and now I have become two companies. Deliver me, I pray from the hand of my brother, from the hand of Esau; for I fear him, let he come and attack me and the mother with the children. For You said, I will surely treat you well, and make your descendants as the sand of the sea, which cannot be numbered for multitude" (**Genesis 32:9-12**).

Prayer was Jacob's alternative, and it is our alternative if we would see revival. Prayer is the mightiest weapon that God has ever placed in the hand of man. Prayer sets the power of God in motion. Prayer obtains that power that spoke the worlds into existence, the power of God. Isaiah, the prophet, said of Him: "He spans the heavens with His hands, He weighs the mountain on His scales. He measures the seas in the palm of His hands" (**Isaiah 40:12**). That is our God. He is the one who commanded, "Call to Me, and I will answer you, and show you great and mighty things, which you do not know" (**Jeremiah 33:3**).

We, too, have an adversary. The adversary we face is a common foe, mightier than Esau, and a murderer from the beginning. He is seeking to destroy civilization and is making tremendous headway. He is so powerful that armies and navies, including the atom or nuclear bomb, cannot hurt him. He has the power to deceive the whole world. He is Satan. But he is afraid of a Christian on his knees. In fact, he trembles when he sees the weakest Christian begin to pray. He fears a church on its knees. He cannot stand the force of prayer.

Prayer subdued Esau. "Now Jacob lifted his eyes and looked, and there, Esau was coming, and with him were four hundred men. So he divided the children among Leah, Rachel, and the two maidservants. And he put the maidservants and their children in front, Leah and her children behind, and Rachel and Joseph last. Then he crossed over before them and bowed himself to the ground seven times, until he came near to his brother. But Esau ran to meet him, and embraced him, and fell on his neck and kissed him, and they wept (**Genesis 33:1-4**).

The record is complete. Prayer has always prevailed with God for His people. Prayer is not new. It has always been God's way. From the beginning prayer history recorded in **Genesis 4:26b**, men have been calling on the name of the Lord. The cries of Israel saved them from Egyptian bondage. Three days of fasting and prayer at the command of Esther saved all the Jews from destruction. Prayer on Mount Carmel by one man, Elijah, won the victory over four hundred fifty false prophets of Baal.

The world is at its darkest again. We have tried everything else without success. Let us try prayer. A praying church will be a revived church. The church will never become a praying church until the importance of prayer is recognized and plans are made to bring prayer to a place of prominence in the life of the church.

The church prayer meeting

A basic need is for the church to become a praying church. To bring this about, revival is needed in many churches. A study of the Scriptures confirms the role of the church in the plan of God. There is clearly an expectation set forth for corporate praying. My good friend, the late Armin Gesswein, spent years reminding us that what appears consistently in the New

Testament, our Guidebook, is an emphasis on the church as a local congregation. The church began this wan in Jerusalem on the Day on Pentecost and then continued to mother other churches after its model. The local church is the basic unit for the major working of the Holy Spirit in the New Testament. Thus, we read of the "church at Antioch," "the church at Corinth," "the church at Ephesus, " "the churches of Galatia" and on and on. Finally, we read in **Revelation** seven times, "he who has an ear, let him hear what the Spirit says to the churches." The role of the church is plain. One would think we would wake up and get the message. No instruction from God is plainer than that which calls individual churches to repentance and renewal.

A church is a reflection of the individuals who have banded themselves together, as a local assembly, to function as the body of Christ. Sometimes we forget this basic truth. If there are to be changes in the church, the changes must be in individuals.

One of the most important commands given to the church is contained in an expression that the Lord Jesus Christ gave to His followers just prior to His ascension. He told His disciples that they were to be witnesses to everyone everywhere. Think of the enormity of that mandate. How can this be possible? Jesus quickly answered that query. He told them to be witnesses, but not even to think about it until they received supernatural power. "But you shall receive power when the Holy Spirit has come upon you; and you shall be witnesses to Me in Jerusalem, and in all Judea and Samaria, and to the end of the earth" (**Acts 1:8**). They waited in Jerusalem, praying together in one accord, for ten days. On the day of Pentecost, the Holy Spirit came. The power needed was now available. The early believers began witness and sharing the Gospel—the "good news of the death burial and resurrection of Jesus for our sins (**1 Corinthians 15:1-4**)—and on that one day about three thousand were saved.

Why is power absent today? One reason is that there are no longer viable church prayer meetings. God's call is not only to revival, it is a call to the praying that brings revival to our churches. God works in answer to prayer. John Wesley knew this and declared: "God works only in concert with the praying of His people."

You will remember Elijah's Mt. Carmel confrontation of the evil in his time that was personified in the false prophets of Baal (**1 Samuel 18**). Before he began his work (which was prayer), he took time to rebuild the altar. God's fire is, and has always been, **altar fire**. We must again build up the altars of prayer that are broken down. Only God Himself can send revival, but He has made ample provision for the kind of praying that brings revival. The failure to make prayer the work that comes before all other work explains why we do not have genuine revivals in our churches.

It would be worthwhile for any person interested in a revived church to read through the Book of Acts and see how Jesus planted His church. The message that is written all through that book emphasizes the importance of a praying church. Yet somehow, the modern church has missed the message. Consequently, we miss revival and the powerful working of the Holy Spirit. Frankly, when the Spirit of prayer departs from our churches, the glory of the Lord departs with it. The result is that the world gets into our churches and we begin to see things from man's point of view, instead of God's point of view.

It is important to make the distinction between praying for a general, widespread spiritual awakening in the land and a specific local revival in a congregation. If you want to see revival in the land, start praying for revival in your church. The reality is that the only thing that Jesus left on earth, when He ascended to His position of glory and authority in Heaven at the right hand of His Father was a praying church with only a small number in attendance. Look at the book of Acts to see the accomplishments of the prayer meetings.

Praying down a revival

Revival in our churches is as near as our prayer meetings. Not only Scripture, but church history itself, shows that no revival or spiritual awakening has ever come any other way. Do we really want a revival in our day as we often profess? If we do, we must repent and establish biblical priorities for our work. We must lay aside our procrastination and begin to build up the prayer live of our churches in every way—personal prayer lives, prayer partner praying, family altars, cottage prayer meetings, church prayer meetings. A revival must be prayed down.

Do you want a revival? You must have an encounter with God. Someone has said that the beginning point can be simply delineated. Draw a circle. Kneel down in the circle. Pray for revival to begin in the circle. Pray that revival will begin with you. The gospel song has the right focus: "not my brother, nor my sister, but it is me, O Lord, standing in the need for prayer." Ask the Holy Spirit to turn His spotlight on your heart. See yourself as God sees you. Follow David's example and ask God to show you any sin that is in your heart (**Psalm 139:23-24**).

Others may know see your sins, but God does. Once He brings conviction, repent and confess. Then you will have forgiveness and cleansing (**1 John 1:9**). It is then that you will be on praying ground. You will then be in a position to participate in a church prayer meeting.

Corporate praying

For almost a quarter of a century, I have had a burning burden to teach God's children basic truths related to praying. God has opened doors around the world for me to do so. The emphasis of the prayer seminar ministry, however, has been on individual, not corporate praying. My regret is that I did not discern that there is a "next step" needed after the individual learns to pray. The individual needs to become part of a church prayer meeting. My efforts during the days ahead will be to bridge the gap between individual praying and church praying. Once this is accomplished, I firmly believe that revival will come.

Study Nineteen

How a church can fulfill its purpose

The Scripture is very clear on Christ's purpose for His church. From the Scripture, we must learn what is expected of the church on earth and then commit ourselves to following God's directions. It is clear, from Scripture, that the early church gathered (not in church buildings constructed for that purpose), but often in homes for worship and instruction. Teaching, preaching, singing, and magnifying Jesus occurred during these public gatherings. Much insight related to these worship/teaching services can be gained by studying **1 Corinthians 14**, as Paul discusses this topic with Corinthian believers.

The public meetings were led by believers who could be termed the pastoral or teaching team in the church, which is those days included what Peter Masters, pastor, Metropolitan Tabernacle, London, refers to as the "prophets" and "junior prophets (the tongues-speakers)" who functioned along side the pastors and teachers. These brethren constituted the platform part, and led the worship in accordance with Paul's rules in an ordered, prearranged, premeditated, and harmonious service in according with the strong terms used in **1 Corinthians 14:33, 40**: "For God is not the author of confusion but of peace, as in all the churches of the saints ... Let all things be done decently and in order." As pastor of a Baptist church that follow congregational government with what is called periodic "business meetings," I often instructed the people that two rules should guide us: first, do all things in love and second, do all things in order. The same principles were to guide the worship/teaching services. Certainly, the pattern that Paul laid out for the Corinthian church is the pattern to be followed today, as it was in the beginning.

Some local churches gather the saints for two meetings on the Lord's Day (Sunday, the first day of the week, the day the early church gathered) for a public/formal worship/teaching service. For well over one hundred years, a teaching period, known as Sunday school, has been included in the schedule, usually convening an hour before the morning worship service. By the way, it is obvious that a Sunday school helps a church fulfill its teaching responsibility. In the long term, the results of gathering men, women, youth, boys and girls together will produce a strong, growing church. Neglecting Bible study will likely result in an anemic, powerless church. It has been my experience that a local church that wishes to grow is wise to use its Sunday school. Historically, many dynamic churches looked upon the evening service as an evangelistic service with an effort to bring unsaved people together to hear the Gospel.

For some churches, there is another service during the mid-week period. This has been what is known as the traditional prayer meeting service. An examination of these services (usually held on Wednesday or Thursday evenings) will verify that the bulk of the time is used for another Bible study and receiving/commenting on prayer requests, with little praying. Consequently, the term "prayer meeting" does not fit. Combining the weekly prayer meeting with a Bible study is obviously better than having no prayer meeting at all. However, Charles Spurgeon was strongly critical of this arrangement, which was a new habit in Victorian times. He could not understand why churches would want to do this, and asked how a combined meeting could do justice to either purpose. Church leadership, who make plans related to the church schedule, would do well to consider Spurgeon's injunction.

The missing element

My friend, the late Dr. Armin Gesswein, was quick to point out in his messages and writings that the only thing that Jesus left on earth, when He returned to His place of honor and glory in Heaven, was a praying church. What about that statement? Is praying our legacy today? When Jesus said, "My house shall be called a house of prayer for all nations," was He talking only to churches during the early years?

As one studies the history of the church, he can only wonder what happened to the prayer meeting. In order to grasp the unique place of a church prayer meeting, it will be helpful to focus on the two distinct types of services set out in the Scripture followed by a local church. Above, I have discussed the worship/teaching service (public/formal). However, there was another kind of meeting or gathering in the New Testament churches, the prayer meeting.

What was the nature of the prayer meetings? A study of the Scripture will give us the answer. In summary, the prayer meeting was less public and probably less formal. No teaching element is reflected. Those attending were believers, often called together by way of response to some pressing crisis. Both men and women participated. By tracing the history of this meeting, held specifically for prayer, we will see how different it was in character from the worship-teaching services. Our study will begin in the book of Acts. Once we discern the pattern, we will study the principle of shared prayer between ordinary believers established by the Lord Jesus Christ in **Matthew 18:19-20**, which we looked at in the beginning of this study.

We will need to study the principle of agreement, which requires unity among the believers. Every church that I know needs a fresh encounter with God. The theology of prayer has been with the Church from her early beginnings. The value of prayer has been preached again and again; our responsibility to pray has been heralded until most Christians live in a failure complex about their prayer lives. Frankly, we give lip service to prayer far more than we give our lips to the service of prayer. We talk about prayer more than we talk to God in prayer.

It is obvious that discipline is required for an individual to enter into the intimate fellowship with God that prayer offers, for which our spirits yearn. It is just as obvious that our soul rebels at the discipline required to enter into that level of communion. Like the dieter who just cannot maintain the necessary self-control to lose weight, we Christians fall into and out of prayer patterns with disappointing regularity. Is it possible that we need the undergirding help of others who are facing the same conflict? If Weight Watchers can help dieters and Alcoholics Anonymous can assist drinkers back to a life of sobriety, isn't if possible that corporate prayer could help believers take and maintain the step out of the guilt that the sin of prayerlessness brings into the glory of a life of prayer? I think so.

But discipline is required for a church to develop a service of corporate praying. There are some biblical principles that are practical and workable. During the next study, we will move forward into the study. My prayer is that many churches will give as much attention and effort to the prayer meeting as they do the worship/teaching service. Once we make the decision that a prayer meeting is needed, establish a program with specific goals and implement the program, we will once again experience the power of a praying church.

We are in trouble as a nation today, but this is not the only time we have been in trouble as a study of our history will reveal. Spiritual conditions were so low in the early 1800s that a Supreme Court Justice is reported to have told pastors in Virginia that the church had no influence at all. Drunkenness was rampant. A spiritual awakening came in 1857-58. Through the research efforts of the late J. Edwin Orr, we can study the elements that brought about the spiritual awakening. Why has there been no similar outpouring of the Spirit of God? Perhaps it is because the people of God have ignored the basic elements that brought about the awakening. Prayer is the work that must come before all other work (**John 14:12-14**). Is our impotence today due to our failure, in our individual lives and in our churches, to understand this basic truth? As we study together, my prayer is that the Holy Spirit, who is our Teacher, will show us truths, and how to implement them, that will make a difference. I want my church to be a praying church. We are living in the Church Age. This is the period that was initiated at Pentecost when Peter used the "keys of the kingdom" to open the door for believing Jews.

Prayer meetings in the Book of Acts

A prayer meeting first appears in **Acts** shortly before Pentecost. It was the gathering of disciples in an upper room in Jerusalem. The account of the upper room prayer meeting is as follows: "These all continued with one accord in prayer and supplication, with the women and Mary the mother of Jesus, and with His brothers" (**Acts 1:14**).

The next recorded prayer meeting is in **Acts 4:24**, when Peter and John reported to the disciples how the chief priests had commanded them not to speak in the name of Jesus. Faced with a serious threat to the testimony, they joined together in prayer.

The same thing happened fourteen years later when Herod arrested Peter and prayer was made without ceasing by the church for him (**Acts 12:5**). "Many" gathered at the house of Mary, the mother of John Mark, for a prayer meeting. Intense prayer was made by the church for Peter "without ceasing." Dr. R. A. Torrey translated "without ceasing" as literally meaning "stretched-out-ed-ly." This represents the soul on the stretch of earnest and intense desire. This is a reminder that prayer is not a leisure enterprise, but is work. When the church gathers for corporate praying, prayer obviously will include worship (seeking God's face), confessing of specific sins, thanksgiving for His blessings, but it must also include work (seeking God's hand). Prayer is work, and without prayer as the foundation, all other efforts that are made for the Lord are unlikely to prevail. God's hand moved in response to the praying of the church. Prayer fetched Peter out of the prison; the angel fetched Peter who was soon knocking on the door where the church was praying. "Many" gathered for the prayer meeting—a great rebuke to numerous believers today. By practice, by conviction, and by instinct, the church gathered together to pray for great matters. Here was a crowded meeting, continuing well after midnight, with both men and women. The early church certainly knew that Jesus had ordained corporate prayer for all.

Principle of shared praying

The principle of shared praying between ordinary believers is supremely established by the Lord Jesus Christ in His very well-known words: "Again, I say to you that if two of you agree on earth concerning anything they ask, it will be done for them by My Father in heaven. For where two or three are gathered together in My name, I am in the midst of them" (**Matthew 18:19-20**). Agreement is impossible with fewer than two. There is a special promise when the smallest plural company possible—two people. There is special power in the prayer of God's people when they are assembled together. We are promised a special hearing when we *agree* about anything we shall ask.

In the next study, we will study the form of praying to which Jesus attached special promises. Once we understand the power of agreement, we will see the power of corporate praying—the church prayer meeting—in a new light. God's people are interested in a revived church, which will never, never become reality until we understand and follow the principle of shared praying.

Study Twenty

Throughout the nation, many sincere and dedicated church leaders are rethinking the approach used in "doing church." Many are exploring new ways that seem strange to those of us who have grown accustomed to certain basics. Their rationale is to appeal to people in what is acknowledged as the "post-Christian era," a time when Christianity no longer exercises a prevailing influence on the mind and heart of our culture. The path of relevancy is being followed to the end that this present generation will have its needs met.

During my lifetime, which will soon span seven decades, I have witnessed many fundamental changes in our culture that have slowly, but surely, impacted the church. In the early years of my life, the Bible had a central place in the curriculum of the public schools and institutions of higher education cultivated the values set out in the Bible. Average Christians serving in elected offices knew their Bibles well enough that biblical teaching had a strong influence on their decision-making. There was no doubt that Christianity shaped the social, political, moral, religious, and intellectual landscape of America. No longer is this true. The present culture is more and more characterized by narcissism, worship of self, and relativism, the denial of absolute morality. Starting in the 60s, the traditional American culture has been under attack. One needs only to spend a few minutes before a television set, watching the programs, to see how far we have drifted. The breakdown in marriage and family continues to be flaunted openly. The disregard for human life in the womb is unabated with abortion on demand the norm.

Narcissism is infatuation with the self. We are in an era of radical selfishness and unbridled individualism. At the same time, there is a rejection of absolute truth, contained in God's Word. Reality depends upon one's own perspective or point of view. The only absolute is that there are no absolutes. One's worldview is simply his own option. In the early years of the twenty-first centur, we appear to be living in the times that the apostle Paul describe for young Timothy when he said: "There will be terrible times in the last days. People will be lovers of self...lovers of pleasure rather than lovers of God...For the times will come when men will not put up with sound doctrine" (**2 Timothy 3:1, 2a, 4b; 4:3a**). What Paul said serves as an apt description of our own narcissistic and relativistic age, when people serve themselves and are increasingly skeptic of the possibility of truth. It is to this new generation that the church is making an attempt to be relevant.

Regardless of the times, it is clear that the Lord Jesus Christ established the church to function as His body on earth to do the things that He would be doing if He were here in the flesh. He, Himself, is the head and believers make up the body. A few years ago, a gospel song was written that contained a striking phrase, "Let the church be the church." One helpful metaphor for the church is "a city on a hill" that "cannot be hidden."

There was a time when America demonstrated, in key areas, the Christian ethos. During the late President Ronald Reagan's funeral service, Associate Justice Sandra O'Connor read a sermon that reflected the desire of our founding fathers that the new nation would be a "city on a hill," certainly drawn from Jesus' words in the Sermon on the Mount: "A city on a hill cannot be hidden" (**Matthew 5:14**). The idea was to establish a community for Christ and His kingdom. There is absolutely no doubt that our fundamental notions of freed and justice came from the bedrock of biblical truth.

The church prayer meeting

We all know that the church needs to walk a biblical path that includes proclamation of the Gospel (proclaiming the saving work of our crucified and risen Lord, Jesus Christ), worship (focusing on our holy God), fellowship (reaching out in Christ's love to care for one another), and evangelism (sharing the Good News with the people of the world). There are numerous ways to express these points in a mission statement. The amazing thing is that most mission statements say nothing about the work that must come before all the other work, and that is prayer. The Lord Jesus Christ was careful to convey this truth in His "greater works" statement (**John 14:12-14**). He did say that the disciples would do greater works, but it would be based on prayer, asking things in Jesus' name. Prayer is the work that must come before all other work in the church. That is a settled truth declared by the Sovereign (the One who has final say). Why do we fail to see that prayer must be included in the mission statement of the church? Could it be because Satan knows that the battle is fought in the place of prayer and wants to keep us from engaging in the battle that leads to his defeat—every time? Prayer must be placed in a preeminent position. Satan always maneuvers to put other things concerning the Lord before prayer and to place prayer at the very last. We need to be reminded that our central service is prayer.

In earlier studies, we have given attention to the need for revival in our churches. A praying church will be a revived church. The purpose this study is to continue our effort to inspire a greater sense of the importance of prayer meetings as a major element of the church. Charles Spurgeon certainly captured the common attitude in churches when he chose the title of his famous exhortation to prayer, **Only a Prayer Meeting!**, which I pointed out in **Study Thirteen**. Why, he inquired, do many believers fail to grasp the momentous significance of the prayer meeting in the work of the church? This continues to be the pressing question that faces the churches and the individual Christians in the churches.

The prayer meeting, without question, is the least regarded gathering in the church program. Pastors frequently complain that most members never attend, while others are more often absent than present. The facetious thing, however, is that most believers, at least at a theoretical level, agree that the prayer meeting is the "power-house" of the church. But how many really think this is so? If they did, all church prayer meetings would be packed.

Why does the Lord want us to pray together? Is the church prayer meeting a biblical duty, or is it to be considered optional. What difference does it make whether we pray privately or with other believers? Will an undersized prayer meeting blight the work of an otherwise vibrant church?

The principle of shared prayer between ordinary believers is supremely established by the Lord Jesus Christ in His very well-known words: "Again I say unto you, that if two of you shall agree on earth as touching any thing that they shall ask, it shall be done for them of My Father which is in heaven" (**Matthew 18:19-20**). We do well to focus on this key passage to understand the special privileges and rules of church prayer meetings.

What form should the prayer meeting ideally take? What should be the style and content of prayer? We will use two Old Testament texts as the starting point. Then, we will move to the Lord's command for corporate praying to complete the study.

Two prophetic Old Testament passages

The first Old Testament text is **Isaiah 56:7**, which is a prophetic text on the subject of corporate praying. God states that the future Gospel-age church will be characterized by communal praying: "For mine house shall be called an house of prayer for all nations [people]." This is clearly about when Gentiles will hear the Word and be converted. The Lord says that they will rejoice "in My house of prayer." It is the will of our Lord and Redeemer that His people be characterized by their praying together. The Lord presents the ministry of corporate praying as an outstanding sign that people have been truly converted. What will be the best evidence of conversion in Gospel days? The churches will be known for their prayer. The Lord said that believers will flock to pray and it will bring them great pleasure and assurance.

Ezekiel 36:37 is the second Old Testament text that sheds light of corporate praying. "Thus saith the Lord God; I will yet for this be enquired of by the house of Israel, to do it for them; I will increase them with men like a flock." Thus, a prophecy is given about how God will work in the church age, which is the Gospel age. He will bless His people with many converts—provided they pray. Without the prayers of the house of Israel, symbolizing the people of God moving together, He will not bless them. "Ye have not," says James, because you ask not" (**James 4:2b**). It is important for us to know that the Lord longs to honor our evangelistic efforts. The lack of prayer is clearly an obstacle that will cause Him to hold back His blessing. When there are no converts in the church, we should ask,, "Have we pleaded with Him in prayer for give us souls.

It is the business of the Christian to pray for the blessing of God upon the work of the church in heralding forth the Gospel. But this text shows that God's people must also prayer as a "house." Praying together must be the business of a church assembly, the people gathered together. We must pray as a body. The **Ezekiel** text shows that the prayer of the group is particularly vital in bringing people to Christ and to His church. Prayer of the group is particularly instrumental. *Israel* must pray for Israel's blessing. To carry this over to our day, the *congregation* must pray for the *congregation*.

Few believers, including church leaders, appreciate the spiritual uniqueness and the importance of church prayer meetings. The uniqueness is not merely a matter of arithmetic. If it were, we can surmise that if one person can be effective in prayer, then a number of people will do even better. A prayer meeting, therefore, cannot be looked upon as merely a multiplicity of people joining forces to increase prayer strength. The idea that what one can do, two can do better is not the mindset in understanding corporate prayingt.

A fundamental principle

Here is one of the fundamental principles of Scripture that all believers should grasp. The principle is that Almighty God, for His own reasons, has ordained the practice of communal, corporate prayer as a duty for His people and has attached unique promises to this duty. Is my church truly a house of prayer? Is the prayer work in my church fulfilling the Lord's express desire that we should labor with Him in prayer?

One can look at the literal sense behinds those beautiful, revealing words: "I will yet...be enquired of...." The Hebrew meaning is helpful in grasping this truth: "I will yet be tracked, pursued, searched after." This kind of praying is not easily accomplished. Rather, great effort and earnestness is suggested in the Hebrew text. The Lord must be asked with persistence on our part. The sense of pursuing and persuading is here. The Lord requires His people to desire very greatly the things for which they pray, and to plead for them.

Christians know that God is a sovereign God, which means that He has final say. Based on this understanding, many believers think that they should pray only one prayer—that God's will be done. They do not feel that their prayers will make any6 difference. Surely, they say, if it is God's will that a sick believer die, he will die. If God has decided to save a person, he will be saved.

In spite of the difficulty in understanding it, the truth is that God urges and commands us to pray and assures us that our prayers will make a difference. The God Who calls His children to pray will not ignore their prayers. Our praying is a part of His glorious plan. God's children have an amazing privilege. They have access to the eternal throne. They may prevail upon their heavenly Father. His ear is always open to their cry. From the very beginning, God's intention is for His children to call upon Him. Prayer history started when the people "began to call upon the name of the Lord" (**Genesis 6:26b**). Prayer, especially corporate prayer, is truly instrumental in the work of God.

Every great blessing in the life of a church and in the life of an individual is obtained in prayer. The failure of the church, today, is the failure of prayer. The failure of the individual Christian is the failure of prayer. Even salvation, initiated and accomplished by a sovereign work of the Holy Spirit, is not consciously tasted without prayer. The Spirit regenerates us, inclines our will, and brings us to the place of repentance. It is all a work of grace. If God did not perform that work within us, we would never desire or seek Him. And yet, in the mystery of His will, He works in such a way that we voluntarily, freely, longingly cry out for pardon and a new life. But for God's regenerating work, we would never ask. And without asking, salvation would never be ours.

Every great blessing must be asked for before it can be received. This principle is illustrated throughout the Bible, which is the record of people in deed need crying out to the Lord for deliverance and received His blessing. It was when God's children saw their need and cried out to God for deliverance that He acted both in Egypt and in Israel, during the day of the judges. The children of Israel sighed by reason of their bondage, and their cry came up to God. He caused them, stubborn and stiff-necked as they were, to cry out pleading for help. Moses prayed, and cried earnestly, and what was the result? The waters of the Red Sea parted before the people. Elijah cried for rain, and it came. Throughout church history, the story is the same. All the great awakenings and reformations have begun with the Lord waking up souls to pray for these things.

We make many mistakes in the Christian life, but the worst is to leave out prayer because then we cannot receive any great blessings. Without prayer, individual believers lack any deep experience of God, and any significant interventions in their lives. What is true of individuals is true of churches as well: no prayer, no blessings. It is true that where there is much prayer, there will be much power; some prayer, some power; no prayer, no power. That is the way that it is without equivocation.

The key New Testament passage

The most direct passage of all on the subject of corporate prayer is the great promise of Christ recorded in **Matthew 18:19-20**). Though expressed as a promise, it is really a command and a directive. The Lord said: "I say unto you, that if two of you shall agree on earth as touching any thing that they shall ask, it shall be done for them of my Father which is in heaven. For where two or three are gathered in my name, there am I in the midst of them." The context of the Lord's declaration was His instruction to the disciples about church affairs, particularly the procedure for dealing with misconduct in the church. He was not speaking to a casual handful of believers, as though giving an optional prayer opportunity to those wishing to meet informally, although His promise most certainly covers such occasions. He was giving official instructions to His churches. He was inaugurating the duty of corporate prayer. It is clear that He is not speaking about a worship service, with preaching, but about a prayer meeting. He said that whatever the church would pray for in a united way, however few the members going down to two persons, their prayers would be heard by the Father, and Christ would be in their midst.

This promise had an immediate application to the matter at hand—discipline in the church body. Whenever a congregation needed guidance to deal with a lapse of godliness, then God would help them if they prayed. However, the words of Christ are by no means limited to the subject of offenses and discipline. They apply to "any thing that they shall ask." The promise covers all the needs of the church.

There is special power in the prayer of God's people when they are assembled together. The promise is made to the smallest plural company possible—two persons. Each word from the mouth of the Lord Jesus Christ is an infallible utterance. He said what He meant and means what He says. We are promised a special hearing when we *agree* about anything we shall ask.

It will be encouraging to review what we have shared in earlier studies about the word *agree* that is used here since it is a Greek word of enormous significance. The Greek word is *sumphoneo*, which literally means to sound together, which is the briefest way to translate it. The Lord said, "If any two of you shall sound together..." *Agree* is an acceptable translation, but the word goes far deeper than that. It is word used to describe musical instruments playing harmoniously together. The word is used, also, in the New Testament to describe the way in which two people verbally strike a bargain. An example is the vineyard parable when the keeper of the vineyard *agrees* with the laborers (Matthew 20:). They bartered and then came to an agreement audibly.

When used about prayer, *agree* refers to prayers spoken aloud, audible praying, not silent praying. It is not a matter of different people praying aloud at the same time, because there can be no intelligent agreement in that. In the "sounding together" image, one prayers and the others follow silently, winging those desires heavenward along with the one who prays aloud. The Lord's people subordinate themselves to one another, and lead one another in prayer. Upon such prayer, there is promised the unique favor of God.

Agreement obviously implies more than the act of following one another's audible prayers. The instrumentalists in an orchestra cannot play together without prior agreement about what they will play. Equally, agreement in prayer extends

147

backwards to before the praying begins. A church prayer meeting is not a time for surprises, shocks, novelties, and innovations. It is not an opportunity for individuals to bang particular drums, or promote causes that may not be in accord with the concerns of the whole prayer meeting. It is certainly not a time for the airing of complaints. This is a gather in which we will be agreed. We will have an "agenda" to guide us emanating from common desires. We pray in agreement for those things. Agreement must be the controlling principle of the occasion. Heaven is waiting for church on earth to ask in agreement.

There are times when believers gather for prayer that some enterprising person thinks it is an ideal time to introduce to the church some unheard-of idea of his own, or even to reprove (in prayer, of course) the people of God, or to protest about something. Clearly, all of this is out of order because the aim is to be at one in the things for which we are praying. When someone feels there is a problem in the church, or is burdened about some new thing that could be done, the matter should be taken up with the officers of the church in the proper way, and not catapulted directly into the prayer meeting.

My prayer, in presenting these studies on a praying church, is that what is said will help the readers to build churches that will glorify God, magnify the Lord Jesus Christ, and operate under the unction of the Holy Spirit, which, like a "city on a hill," cannot be hidden to the world. We need the Lord to enlighten our eyes that we may comprehend afresh the importance of prayer and know anew its value. We have all committed the sin of neglecting prayer. It is time to repent and put prayer in the place that God has intended it to be both in individual lives and in the life of the church.

Study Twenty-one

The most needed work today is prayer work, which is virtually absent in many local churches. Instead of placing the emphasis where Jesus directed, attention is given in many churches to praise and worship, with some proclamation included. Why is prayer so important? John Wesley observed, "God works only in concert with the praying of His people." One need only read Jesus' words to His disciples in the Upper Room in what I call "the Greater Works" passage to see the centrality that must be given to prayer: "Most assuredly, I say to you, he who believes in Me, the works that I do he will do also; and greater works than these he will do, because I go to My Father. And whatever you ask in My name, that I will do, that the Father may be glorified in the Son. If you ask anything in My name, I will do it" (**John 14:12-14**).

We can only imagine what greater works would be than those performed by the Lord Jesus Christ when He was on earth. Not only were His words gracious, His works were profound. Is it possible that there could be greater works than those that Jesus performed? One thing that we can count on is that His Word is dependable. Jesus said what He meant and meant what He said. Therefore, greater works than what was being done when He was on earth are possible.

"Greater works than these," Jesus said. But don't stop reading there or you will not have a clue as to what He meant. He said that as "you ask in My name," greater works will be done. Asking in His name is prayer. Only as prayer is made in His name will greater works transpire. His name is His authority for blessings to be released from God's storehouse. Asking in His name mandates knowing His mind on a matter. A warning is given that it is possible to pray, even sincerely, and not receive an answer. We must come with the right motive, otherwise we are asking amiss (**James 4:3**). The right motive is that God will receive glory from the answer that is forthcoming to our requests. When the motive is not right, you can say "Jesus" ten thousand times, but God will not hear the prayer.

Prayer work

Prayer is the work that must come before all other work. Why is this true? A study of the Scriptures reveals that the Sovereign God (the one who has final say) has ordained it to be so. The parameters are established already. Until prayer work is done, all other work for the Lord will be rather inconsequential and ineffective. This is a central truth taught in each prayer seminar. Not only does an individual Christian need to become an intercessor, each local congregation needs to become a praying church.

Jack Taylor, a great man of God whose insights into prayer are helpful, has pointed out that "no church's ultimate effectiveness will rise to stay above the level of its corporate prayer life—the praying of its members. No part of a church's ministry will rise to stay above the level of its prayer ministry." He then says: "No church's corporate prayer life will be greater than the personal prayer lives of those who make up its constituency. No believer's prayer life will rise to stay above the level of his or her own personal, regular, daily time of worship with God."

Prayer history begins in **Genesis 4:26b**: "Then began men to call upon the name of the Lord." As centuries rolled along, Israel was back in the land God promised to Abraham. One day during Isaiah's lifetime, God looked down on Israel and "saw that there was no man, and wondered that there was no intercessor" (**Isaiah 59:16**). Conditions, however, were even more serious than failing to pray for others, the observation a little later was that "there is none that calleth upon Thy name, that stirreth himself to lay hold on Thee" (**Isaiah 64:7**). What a contrast from the time when men were calling on the name of the Lord and when none were found calling on His name.

Prayer work beginning in 1857-58

A spiritual awakening came to the United States in 1857-58. Through the research efforts of the late J. Edwin Orr, we can study the elements of the spiritual awakening. During the past few years, I have read and reread Dr. Orr's book entitled **The Fervent Prayer** (Chicago: Moody Press, 1974) in which he documents the worldwide impact of the Great Awakening of 1858. A companion to his book, **The Flaming Tongue**, which deals with spiritual awakenings during the early twentieth century, **The Fervent Prayer** covers the revivals of the second half of the nineteenth century—from the awakening that began in the United States and Great Britain about 1857 and extended through the ministry of Dwight L. Moody until 1899.

The Role of Prayer in Spiritual Awakening

In 1979, during the time I was serving as a local church pastor, I learned of the work that Dick Burr was doing providing instruction on prayer. Our church decided to invite him to come and share what God had given him. We invited all the churches in our association to join with us March 19-21, 1980, and many did. During the sessions, Richard introduced J. Edwin Orr and shared a Campus Crusade film with Dr. Orr speaking at the National Prayer Congress, Dallas, Texas, October 26-29, 1976. I was profoundly touched with what I heard and began to pray that God would bring another spiritual awakening in my day. Dr. Orr's message, entitled "The Role of Prayer in Spiritual Awakening," follows:

Dr. A. T. Pierson once said, "There has never been a spiritual wakening in any country or locality that did not begin in united prayer." Let me recount what God has done through concerted, united, sustained prayer.

Not many people realize that in the wake of the American Revolution there was a moral slump. Drunkenness became epidemic. Out of a population of five million, 300,000 were confirmed drunkards: they were burying fifteen thousand of them each year. Profanity was of the most shocking kind. For the first time in the history of the American settlement, women were afraid to go out at night for fear of assault. Bank robberies were a daily occurrence.

What about the churches? The largest denomination was the Methodists and they were losing more members than they were gaining. The second largest was the Baptists and they said they were having their most wintry season. The Presbyterians in general assembly deplored the nation's ungodliness. The Congregationalists were the strongest in New England. In a typical Congregational church, the Rev. Samuel Shepherd of Lennox, Massachusetts in sixteen years had not taken one young person into fellowship. The Lutherans were so languishing that they discussed uniting with Episcopalians who were even worse off. The Protestant Episcopal Bishop of New York, Bishop Samuel Proovost, quit functioning: he had confirmed no one for so long that he decided he was out of work, so he took up other employment. The Chief Justice of the United States, John Marshall, wrote to the Bishop of Virginia, Bishop Madison, that the Church "was too far gone ever to be redeemed." Voltaire averred, and Tom Pain echoed, "Christianity will be forgotten in thirty years."

In case this is thought to be the hysteria of the moment, Kenneth Scott Latourette, the great church historian wrote: "It seem as if Christianity were about to be ushered out of the affairs of men." The churches had their backs to the wall, seeming as if they were about to be wiped out. How did the situation change? It came through a concert of prayer.

I must go back a little. There was a Scottish Presbyterian minister in Edinburgh named John Erskine, who published a Memorial (he called it) pleading with the people of Scotland and elsewhere to unite in prayer for the revival of religion. He sent one copy of this little book to Jonathan Edwards of New England. That great theologian was so moved he wrote a response which grew longer than a letter, so that finally he published it in a book, entitled: "A Humble Attempt to Promote Explicit Agreement and Visible Union of All God's People in Extraordinary Prayer for the Revival of Religion and the Advancement of Christ's Kingdom on earth, pursuant to Scripture Promises and Prophecies concerning the Last Times." That was the title of the book, not the book itself. In those days, a title was a synopsis of what was in the book.

But do not miss its message: "A Humble Attempt" (New England's modesty) "to promote explicit agreement and visible union of God's people in extraordinary prayer for a revival of religion and extension of Christ's Kingdom." Is not this what is missing so much from all our evangelistic efforts—explicit agreement, visible union, unusual prayer?

The movement had started in Britain through William Carey, Andrew Fuller and John Sutcliffe and other leaders who began what the British called "the Union of Prayer." Hence, the year after John Wesley died, the Second Great Awakening began and swept Great Britain. In New England, there was a man of prayer named Isaac Backus, a Baptist pastor, who, in 1794, when conditions were at their worst, sent out an urgent plea for revival to pastors of every Christian denomination in the United States.

Take the liberal arts colleges at that time. A poll taken at Harvard had discovered not one believer in the whole student body. They took a poll at Princeton, a much more evangelical place: they discovered only two believers in the student body, and only five that did not belong to the filthy speech movement of that day. Students rioted. They held a mock communion at Williams College; and they put on anti-Christian plays at Dartmouth. They burned down the Nassau Hall at Princeton. They forced the resignation of the president of Harvard. They took a Bible out of a Presbyterian church in New Jersey, and burned it in a public bonfire. Christians were so few on campus in the 1790s that they met in secret, like a communist cell, and kept their minutes in code so that no one would know what they were doing to persecute them.

Churches knew that their backs were to the wall. So the Presbyterians of New York, New Jersey, and Pennsylvania adopted it for all their churches. Bishop Francis Asbury adopted it for all the Methodists. The Congregational and Baptist Associations, the Reformed and the Moravians all adopted the plan, until America like Britain was interlaced with a network of prayer meetings. They set aside the first Monday of each month to pray. It is not long before the revival came. It broke out first of all in Connecticut, then spread to Massachusetts and all the seaboard states, in every case entirely without extravagance or outcry. Every report mentions this.

However, there were some variations. When the revival reached the frontier in Kentucky, it encountered a people really wild and irreligious. Congress had discovered that in Kentucky there had not been more than one court of justice held in five years. Peter Cartwright, a Methodist evangelist, wrote that when his father settled in Logan County, it was known as Rogues' Harbor. If someone committed a murder in Massachusetts or robbery in Rhode Island, all he needed to do was to cross the Alleghenies. The decent people in Kentucky formed regiments of vigilantes to fight for law and order. They fought a pitched battle with outlaws and lost.

There was a Scotch-Irish Presbyterian minister named James McGready whose chief claim was he was so ugly that he attracted attention. It was reported that people sometimes stopped in the street to ask: "What does he do?" "He's a preacher." Then they reacted, saying: "A man with a face that must really have something to say."

McGready settled in Logan County, pastor of three little churches. He wrote in his diary that the winter of 1799 for the most part was "weeping and mourning with the people of God." It was like Sodom and Gomorrah Lawlessness prevailed everywhere. McGready was such a man of prayer that, not only did he promote the concert of prayer every first Monday of the month, but he got his people to pray for him at sunset on Saturday evening and sunrise Sunday morning. Then in the summer of 1800 came the great Kentucky revival. Eleven thousand people came to a communion service. McGready hollered for help, regardless of denomination. Baptists and Methodists came in response and the great camp meeting revivals started to sweep Kentucky and Tennessee and then spread over North Carolina and South Carolina, and swept the frontier. That was the turning point.

Out of that second great awakening after the death of John Wesley came the whole modern missionary movement and its societies. Out of it came the abolition of slavery, and popular education, Bible societies and Sunday schools, and many social benefits accompanying the evangelistic drive. More than six hundred colleges in the middle West were founded by revivalists.

Conditions deteriorated by the middle of the nineteenth century. Why? It sounds familiar, the country was seriously divided over the issue of slavery; and second, people were making money lavishly and when they do, they turn their backs upon God.

In September 1857, a man of prayer, Jeremiah Lanphier, started a prayer meeting in the upper room of the Dutch Reformed Church Consistory Building, in Manhattan. In response to his advertisement, only six people out of the population of a million showed up. But the following week, there were fourteen, and then twenty-three, when it was decided to meet every day for prayer. By late winter, they were filling the Dutch Reformed Church, then the Methodist Church on John Street, then Trinity Episcopal Church on Broadway at Wall Street. By February 1858, every church and public hall in downtown New York was filled. Horace Greeley, the famous editor, sent a reporter with horse and buggy racing around the prayer meetings to see how many men were praying: in one hour, he could get to only twelve meetings, but he counted 6,100 men attending. Then a landslide of prayer began, which overflowed to the churches in the evenings. People began to be converted, ten thousand a week in New York City alone. The movement spread throughout New England, the church bells bringing people to prayer at eight in the morning, twelve noon, six in the evening. The revival raced up the Hudson and down the Mohawk, where the Baptists, for example, had so many people to baptize that they went down to the river, cut a big hole in the ice, and baptized them in cold water: when Baptists do that they really are on fire.

When the revival reached Chicago, a young shoe salesman went to the superintendent of the Plymouth Congregational Church, and asked if he might teach Sunday School. The superintendent said, "I am sorry, young fellow. I have sixteen teachers too many, but I will put you on the waiting list." The young man insisted: "I want to do something just now." "Well, start a class." "How do I start a class?" "Get some boys off the street, and don't bring them here. Take them out into the country and after a month you will have control of them, then bring them here. They will be your class." He took them to a beach on Lake Michigan and he taught them Bible verses and Bible games; then he took them to the Plymouth Congregational Church. The name of the young man was Dwight Lyman Moody, and that was the beginning of his ministry that lasted forty years.

For instance, Trinity Episcopal Church in Chicago had 121 members in 1857; in 1860, 1400. That was typical of the churches. More than a million people were converted to God in one year out of a population of thirty million. Then that same revival jumped the Atlantic, appeared in Ulster, Scotland and Wales, then England, parts of Europe, South Africa and South India, anywhere there was an evangelical cause. It sent mission pioneers to many countries. Effects were felt for forty years. Having begun in a movement of prayer, it was sustained by a movement of prayer.

That movement lasted for a generation, but at the turn of the twentieth century, there was need of awakening again. A general movement of prayer began, with special prayer meetings at Moody Bible Institute, at Keswick Convention in England, and places as far apart as Melbourne, Wonsan in Korea, and the Nilgiri Hills of India. So all around the world believers were praying that there might be another great awakening in the twentieth century.

Now, some people say that we are in the midst of another great awakening today. I certainly believe the tide has turned, that we are on the move again, but I do not think that we have reached anything like what God has done in the past. Let me give you examples from the student world.

One of the leaders of the revival of 1905 was a young man called K. S. Latourette, who became the famous professor, Kenneth Scott Latourette. He reported that, at Yale in 1905, 25% of the student body were enrolled in prayer meetings and in Bible study. I live next door to UCLA, which has an enrollment of 36,000, and I do not believe that there are 9,000 enrolled in Campus Crusade, Inter-Varsity and other evangelical groups, or in all the church groups put together. We have not reached that yet.

As far as the churches were concerned, the ministers of Atlantic City reported that, of a population of 50,000, there were only fifty adults left unconverted. Take Portland, Oregon. 240

majors stores closed from 11:00 till 2:00 each day to enable people to attend prayer meetings, signing an agreement so that no one would cheat and stay open. Take First Baptist Church of Paducah, Kentucky: the pastor, was an old man, Dr. J. J. Cheek, took in a thousand members in two months and died of overwork. The Southern Baptists said his was "a glorious ending to a devoted ministry."

That is what was happening in the United States in 1905. But how did it begin? Most people have heard of the Welsh Revival, which started in 1904. It began as a movement of prayer. I knew Evan Roberts personally (of course, I met him thirty years later), a man devoted to God. Seth Joshua, the Presbyterian evangelist, had come to the Newcastle Emlyn College where Evan Roberts was studying for the ministry. Evan Roberts, then 26, had been a coal miner. The students were so moved that they asked if they could attend his next campaign nearby, so they cancelled classes to go to Blaenanerch, where Seth Joshua prayed publicly "O God, bend us." And Evan Roberts went forward, where he prayed with great agony, "O God, bend me."

Upon his return, he could not concentrate on his studies. He went to the Principal Philips of his college, and explained: "I keep hearing a voice that tells me I must go home to speak to our young people in my home church, Mr. Phillips, is that the voice of the devil or the voice of the Spirit?" Principal Phillips answered, very wisely, "The devil never gives orders like that. You can have a week off."

So Evan Roberts went back home to Loughor and announced to the pastor, "I've come to preach." The pastor was not at all convinced, but asked: "How about speaking at the prayer meeting on Monday?" He did not even let him speak to the prayer meeting, but told the praying people, "Our young brother, Evan Roberts, feels he has a message for you, if you care to wait." Seventeen people waited behind and were impressed with the directness of the young man's words. Evan Roberts told his fellow members: "I have a message for you from God. You must confess any known sin to God and put any wrong done to man right. Second, you must put away any doubtful habit. Third, you must obey the Spirit promptly. Finally, you must confess your faith in Christ publicly." And by ten o'clock, all seventeen had responded. The pastor was so pleased that he asked, "How about your speaking at the mission service tomorrow night and the midweek service Wednesday night?" He preached all week, and was asked to stay another week; and then "the break" came.

I have read the Welsh newspapers of the period. In them were snippets of ecclesiastical news, such as: "The Rev. Peter Jones has just been appointed chaplain to the Bishop of St. David's." Very interesting, but not earth-shaking. "Mowbray Street Methodist Church had a very interesting rummage sale." But suddenly there was a headline, "Great Crowds of People Drawn to Loughor." For some days a young man named Evan Roberts was causing great surprise. The main road between Llanelly and Swansea on which the church was situated was packed, wall to wall, people trying to get into the church. Shopkeepers closed early to find a place in the big church.

Now the news was out. A reporter was sent down and he described vividly what he saw, a strange meeting, which closed at 4:25 in the morning, and even then the people did not seem willing to go home. They were still standing in the street outside the church, talking about what had taken place. There was a very British summary: "I felt that this was no ordinary gathering." The news was out. Next day, every grocery shop in that industrial valley was emptied of groceries by people attending the meetings, and on Sunday, every church was filled. The movement went like a tidal wave over Wales, in five months there being a hundred thousand people converted throughout the country. Five years later, Dr. J. V. Morgan wrote a book to debunk the revival, his main criticism that, of a hundred thousand joining the churches in five months of revival excitement, after five years only 80,000 still stood in the membership of those churches.

It was the social impact that was astounding. For example, judges were presented with white gloves, not a case to try: no robberies, no burglaries, no rapes, no murders, and no embezzlements, nothing. District councils held emergency meetings to discuss what to do with the police now that they were unemployed. In one place, the sergeant of the police was sent for, and asked, "What do you do with your time?" He replied, "Before the revival, we had two main jobs, to prevent crime and to control crowds, as at football games. Since the revival started, there is practically no crime. So we just go with the crowds." A councillor asked: "What does that mean?" The sergeant replied: "You know where the crowds are. They are packing out the churches." "But how does that affect the police?" He was told: "We have seventeen police in our station, but we have three quartets; and if any church wants a quartet to sing, they simply call the police station."

As the revival swept Wales, drunkenness was cut in half. There was a wave of bankruptcies, but nearly all taverns. There was even a slowdown in the mines. You say, "How could a religious revival cause a strike?" It did not cause a strike, but just a slowdown, for so many Welsh coal miners were converted and stopped using bad language that the horses that dragged the trucks in the mines could not understand what was being said to them. Hence transportation slowed down for a while until they learned the language of Canaan. When I first heard that story, I thought that was a tall tale, but I can document it, even from Westminster Abbey.

That revival also affected sexual moral standards. I had discovered through the figures given by British government experts that, in Radnorshire and Merionethshire, the actual illegitimate birth rate had dropped 44% within a year of the beginning of the revival. That revival swept Britain. It so moved all of Norway that the Norwegian Parliament passed special legislateion to permit laymen to conduct Communion because the clergy could not keep up with the number of the converts desiring to partake. It swept Sweden, Finland and Denmark, Germany, Canada from coast to coast, all of the United States, Australia, New Zealand, South Africa, East Africa, Central Africa, West Africa, North Africa, touching also Brazil, Mexico, and Chile ...yet until 1973, the extent of that revival was unknown until I published my book, **The Flaming Tongue**.

As always, it began through a movement of prayer, with prayer meetings all over the United States as well as the other countries, and soon there came the great time of the harvest. So what is the lesson we can learn? It is a very simple one. Its that familiar text, "If My people called by My name will humble themselves, pray, and seek My face, and turn from their wicked ways, I will then hear from Heaven, will forgive their sin, and heal their land" (**2 Chronicles 7:14**).

What's involved in this? God expects us to pray. But we must not forget what Jonathan Edwards said: "promote explicit agreement and visible union of all God's people in extraordinary prayer." What do we mean by extraordinary prayer? When you find people getting up at 6 o'clock in the morning to pray or having a half night of prayer to midnight, that's extraordinary praying. When they give up their lunch hour to attend a prayer meeting, that's extraordinary prayer. "United and concerted" doesn't mean that a Baptist becomes any less of a Baptist or an

Episcopalian is any less loyal to the Thirty-nine Articles or a Presbyterian turns his back on the Westminster Confession—not at all. But they recognize each other as brothers and sisters in Christ and are prepared to pray together in concerted prayer that God may hear and answer.

We haven't reached that yet, but this National Conference on Prayer is unprecedented in some ways. It is a sign of the direction in which we are moving. Now those of us who are here must take this challenge to your churches. When they are prepared to set aside time to pray for spiritual awakening, that is when God is going to answer. .

Some may say, "Then it is up to us." That isn't true either. Matthew Henry said that "When God intends great mercy for His people, He first of all sets them to praying."

Even God is sovereign in this matter, but we must respond. He has never chosen never to work without our cooperation. So whether your interpretation of revival is either Calvinistic or Arminian, it is a very a simple thing. You must pray. May God help us so to pray. Amen.

Spiritual famine in the land

Why has there been no similar outpouring? Perhaps, it is because the people of God have ignored the basic elements that brought the awakening. Generally, the needed prayer work is not being done. When it is, we see God's hand moving as He did in the past.

As we look around us, we see the need for a return to the Christian values that characterized our nation just a few years ago. Most Americans realized that very need the hours after 9/11. Even members of the Congress joined together on the Capitol steps to sing "God Bless America."

God's plan to redeem the world is for the church to prevail against the gates of hell (**Matthew 16:18**). Paul's clarion call to the church at Rome is the call to the church today: "The hour has come for you to wake up from your sleep" (**Romans 13:11**). For the church to wake up, it is essential that individual believers wake up. Every church needs a fresh encounter with God.

Prayer is not new and has been a key element in the work of the church since it was founded. The value of prayer has been emphasized in sermons again and again. In fact, our responsibility to pray has been heralded until most Christians live with a failure complex about their prayer lives. There is no doubt about it. We give lip service to prayer in our churches more than we give our lips to the service of prayer. Most of us talk about prayer more than we talk to God in prayer. The need is pressing for us to change.

A genuine prayer meeting

For over 1400 Sundays, I had the privilege to serve Baptist churches as pastor. Other than seven years at Kerby Knob Baptist Church in Kentucky's Appalachia region, the weekly schedule included what we called the "prayer meeting"—a mid-week service held on Wednesday nights. Due to distance, our work schedules, the ages of our children, Kerby Knob replaced the prayer meeting with a Saturday night preaching service.

It was only during the last two years of my pastor ministry that I learned the difference in what we had been doing on Wednesday nights and a genuine prayer meeting. Time was used in the earlier mid-week services for a Bible study. During the service, we shared prayer requests, which often took more of our time than actual praying. By the time we sung a few songs, shared a Bible study, and received prayer requests, there was no time left to pray.

During the last two years of my pastoral ministry, I began to learn about the purpose and power of prayer in an individual's Christian life. My understanding of the place of corporate prayer began to broaden.

I had already learned that the mid-week service should not be termed the "prayer meeting." Instead, we listed it in the bulletin as the "mid-week service" as a matter of integrity.

Why not make the mid-week service a prayer meeting? And that is what we did. No singing and no Bible study were included. No prayer requests were offered. Those gathered for the prayer meeting just prayed. To get prayer requests before us, the church office prepared a prayer sheet on Wednesday afternoon. Members were instructed to call in requests by 3 p.m. in order to have them on the prayer sheet. When special situations arose after the prayer sheets were prepared, a board was provided to enable anyone to share last minute requests. Further, we taught the people to use the actual praying to bring up new requests. Since one of the rules of the prayer meeting is praying in agreement (literally make the same sound), this type of sharing prayer and praying for prayer requests meets the parameters of praying in agreement.

Since the church was located in an urban area, a supper was provided beginning at 5:30 p.m. This enabled families to come immediately after work. Attendance was excellent. At 6:15 p.m., everyone gathered in the auditorium. Prayer groups of five were formed throughout the auditorium. No leaders were designated. No one called the meeting to order. Folks began to pray immediately. Someone began calling on the Lord. Others followed. Since an hour was designated, it was common that each person prayed more than once. The prayer meeting ended around 7:15 p.m. Other than the nurseries and children's ministries, no other activities were scheduled that would compete with the prayer meeting. At 7:30 p.m., other activities were available, such as committee meetings or deacons' meetings, There was choir practice. Some members visited homes or the hospitals before going home. Since we felt that families needed to spend time together, no other night meetings were scheduled during the week.

Upon leaving that pastorate to assume responsibilities as president of a Bible college, I made the following observation:

During my last two years as a pastor, I had the privilege of baptizing over one hundred people each year. Others were saved who became members of other churches. Certainly, this was the most fruitful era of my twenty-seven years as a pastor. In looking back, I believe that there were two basic elements that were different from the other twenty-five years. First, we did the prayer work that must always be done before other work for the Lord is fruitful. Not only did the people gather for a genuine prayer meeting, we developed the prayer chapel ministry with someone praying in the prayer chapel every hour around the clock. We asked God to turn His eyes upon us and to extend His hand of blessing. Second, we magnified the Lord Jesus Christ. We lifted Him up in our singing, teaching, praying, preaching. When the Lord Jesus Christ is exalted ("lifted up"), people are drawn to Him. During this time, we had a radio program called "Turning Point." The theme song used to introduce each broadcast was "Turn Your Eyes Upon Jesus." When the church becomes a praying church and when the Lord Jesus Christ is magnified, the Holy Spirit will move in unprecedented ways. He has in the past and will do so in the present.

Prayer seminar helps you get started!

"... I will give myself to prayer ..." **Psalm 109:4b**

Most Christians know the important place of prayer in the life of a believer. I do not have to make a case with you about that.

But it is not easy to pray. It is easier to preach, to do youth work or the work of a deacon, to teach a Sunday school class, or to go visiting! Why is this?

I believe the reason Satan doesn't want a person to learn to pray is because prayer unleashes the power of God in the life of a believer. Satan trembles when he sees the weakest Christian on his knees. I will never win the war if I don't know where the battle is being fought. Prayer is the place!

What about your personal altar? Is it broken down and deserted? Take an inventory of your prayer life. What is happening in your life in answer to prayer? What about others in your church? If you have said, *I want my church to be a praying church!*, a prayer seminar can help your desire to become a reality. Hundreds of churches have found that the **Prayer Seminar** assists in the achievement of this goal.

The **Prayer Seminar** is a six-hour event that can be used with an entire congregation or with smaller groups such as elders, deacons, youth, or leadership. It lends itself to retreat or conference settings. The seminar teaches the importance of a proper and effective prayer life for the Christian and clearly demonstrates the spiritual impact every believer can generate through prayer. Using the *Prayer Seminar Workbook*, a person can learn how to structure daily praying as the guiding foundation and force for his life.

Not only does the prayer seminar stand alone in its impact as a special event, it is excellent preparation for evangelistic efforts, revival meetings, lay witness programs, stewardship emphases (including building programs and budget subscription drives), mission projects, and leadership development focus.

There are several scheduling patterns that can be followed, the most popular being an all-day Sunday seminar (which reaches the most people in a church family, thus assuring the greatest impact). The theme we suggest is **"A Day in Thy Courts"** (**Psalm 84:10**). Saturday seminars are usually from 9:00 a.m. until 4:30 p.m. Another scheduling possibility is Friday night— Saturday morning. Scheduling, however, is flexible to meet the sponsor's needs.

Almost 2,000 seminars have been conducted in forty-seven states, the District of Columbia, and fifty-nine nations: Argentina, Australia, the Bahamas, Botswana, Brazil, Canada, Chile, China, Costa Rica, Cuba, Dominican Republic, England, Fiji Islands, France, Germany, India, Indonesia, Israel, Italy, Jamaica, Japan, Korea, Lesotho, Malaysia, Mexico, Mozambique, Namibia, New Zealand, Nigeria, N. Ireland, Okinawa, Pakistan, Panama, the Philippines, Puerto Rico, Romania, Russia, Scotland, Singapore, South Africa, Sudan, Swaziland, Switzerland, Thailand, Ukraine, Venezuela, and Zambia. The **Prayer Seminar Workbook** has been translated into many languages, including, Spanish, German, Portuguese, Russian, Romanian, Malay, Telugu, Sotho, Thai, Indonesian, Hausa/Fulani, Ibo, Korean, Urdu, Luganda, Swahili, and others.

Seminars have been conducted with Baptists (myriad groups, including churches in the American Baptist Convention, Association of Conservative Baptists, General Baptists, Free Will Baptists, General Association of Regular Baptists, Southern Baptists, and independent Baptists), Christian and Missionary Alliance, Brethren, Free Brethren, Grace Brethren, Free Methodist, Southern Methodist, United Methodist, Nazarene, Presbyterian, Mennonite, Apostolic, Assembly of God, Church of God, Conservative Congregational, Christian, Pentecostal, Evangelical Free, Lutheran, Pentecostal Free Will Baptists, Reformed, Christian Reformed, Quakers (Friends), Salvation Army, and independent Bible churches. In addition, there have been seminars in Bible colleges and liberal arts/colleges/ universities. Prayer seminars have been conducted for statewide men's retreats, summer camp meetings and/or retreats for special groups, such as pastors. Seminars have been conducted on military bases around the world and in prisons.

HOW TO:

- Establish prayer as a daily priority.
- Organize your praying following a biblical pattern.
- Worship, praise, confess, and thank the Lord.
- Pray for yourself, as well as others.

Although Dr. Henry personally has conducted almost eighteen hundred seminars and has logged almost three million miles of travel, he continues as excited about the prayer seminar as he was when the first one was conducted in September, 1980. He wants to share as often and as widely as possible. Please share with others the availability of the prayer seminar. Every church, regardless of size, can have a prayer seminar.

The prayer seminar is a faith ministry that trusts God to provide the financial needs through local churches and individuals. Therefore, we do not charge a set fee. Basically, participants are encouraged to contribute a one-time gift through the church love offering for the seminar as the Lord leads. Each participant receives a copy of the **Prayer Seminar Workbook**, the basic teaching tool. The suggested contribution is $5, to defray the printing cost. Beyond the free-will offering, help with travel is necessary. If the Lord places a desire on your heart to host a seminar, however, do not hesitate to make contact with J. Gordon Henry Ministries about the travel expense, if that is a problem.

Testimonies

Of all the speakers I've heard speak about prayer, no one has touched my heart more than Dr. Henry. He does not come with enticing words, but rather the Word of God. And when he begins speaking on prayer, you begin to sense the Spirit of God moving in and through the congregation and upon people's lives. He just takes you to the Word—the best book on prayer I know."

Dr. John A. Hash, President-Founder
Bible Pathway Ministries
Murfreesboro TN

On behalf of all of us here at Park Avenue, I want to thank you, again, for the blessings of this past Sunday. I believe that it will go down as one of the great days in the history of our church, as far as spiritual growth is concerned. God used you in a mighty way and we give Him the glory for all that He did through you.

Bob Mowrey, Pastor
Park Avenue Baptist Church
Nashville TN

I am unable to find the words to express the joy and deep appreciation for the prayer seminar you conducted in our church Sunday, November 30. I do not believe I have ever attended any seminar, or training conference of any type, that was more helpful to me than your prayer seminar. I am confident I speak for our members, as well.

Joe A. Williams, Pastor
First Baptist Church
Vernon AL

One of the great blessings of our Nigerian Crusade was the prayer seminars conducted by Dr. Henry. Not only were the lives of the Nigerians blessed, the American pastors received a true revival in their lives. The Holy Spirit uses the Word of God in each seminar to make a difference.

Dr. Gene M. Williams, President Emeritus
Luther Rice Seminary
Lithonia GA

I certainly wish to express my appreciation for your coming and sharing the prayer seminar October 5. This seminar has made a difference in my life, my wife's life, and the lives of many people in the congregation. I appreciated the practical handles that you shared which made it helpful to implement prayer in our lives. I've known for years that I ought to pray more. Your practical helps showed me how to do it. Thanks again—keep up this worthwhile ministry.

J. Richard D'Andre, Pastor
Groton Heights Baptist Church
Groton CT

"*I knew that!*" is an often repeated phrase today, and for many a pastor in the prayer seminar, it could be phrased, "*I taught that!*" So often, however, is that "*other voice*" that is heard. Dr. Henry is just such a voice bringing a seminar on prayer that refreshes and revitalizes the weary heart with long-known truths and fresh, exhilarating insights. Our one day with Dr. Henry has changed the prayer lives of our people as God's Word was used to challenge, uplift, exhort, and instruct. Any one of us would do well to give more time to prayer; any church would do well to give one day to prayer with Dr. Henry.

George A. Garancosky, Jr., Pastor
Faith Baptist Church
Beaver Springs PA

What a delight it was to have you share your love for the Lord and the informative prayer seminar. The comments were numerous this year, even more so than last year. Many were moved to grow closer to the Lord and to be consistent in their prayer lives.

Dr. J. Bruce Sofia, Senior Pastor
Gloucester County Community Church
Sewell NJ

Thank you, thank you, thank you—for the prayer seminar. Can people sit for over six hours to be instructed in the work of prayer? They can! Time speeds, interest grows, and conviction comes by the Holy Spirit. Growth and change come out of the Holy Spirit's work as your prayer seminar proceeds. I have heard only positive, and grateful, expressions of appreciation for the changes God has produced. I can say without hesitation that I learned more about prayer in the seminar than I learned in seminary and in over thirty years of pastoral ministry. Your humble help was felt by so many people here. I will pray for you as long as I live, and for your ministry.

Dr. Harris J. Verkaik, Pastor
Calvary Reformed Church
South Holland IL

The spiritual impact of our recent prayer seminar will surely be felt for many weeks to come. Our people are still talking about it and have asked us to schedule another seminar in the near future. The workbook is an excellent learning aid and the study of prayer was one of the most exhaustive studies I have ever had the privilege to encounter. Our people really appreciated the day. I believe the great element of the seminar was your Spirit-filled leadership. God certainly has His hand of blessing upon your life and has equipped you for a unique and much needed ministry. I am happy to recommend you to any church that is serious about the importance of prayer. Thank you for sharing this day with the First Baptist Church family. It was truly a wonderful day!

John W. Fleming, Associate Pastor
First Baptist Church of Perrine
Miami FL

We in missions have long emphasized the vitalness of prayer if we are to be effective in the ministry to which God has called us. At the same time, it is easy to become so involved in ministry that we fail to pray personally as we ought. God uses Dr. Henry in a precious way to drive home this truth. In our opinion, you will not go wrong to schedule a prayer seminar with Dr. Henry at your earliest convenience.

Birne D. Wiley, President
Missionary Tech Team
Longview TX

Indeed, we know that prayer is the hardest work in the ministry. Therefore, it is strategic that in a place such as ours, where we equip full-time servants of Christ, that the students be aware of the greatest source of power, and yet the greatest area of conflict. Thank you, Dr. Henry, for your clear, concise, and convincing seminar that is based on the Word of God, for the honor and glory of Jesus Christ.

Dr. Harry E. Fletcher, President
Washington Bible College
Lanham MD

I would like to introduce the fine ministry of Dr. J. Gordon Henry and his Prayer Seminar to your church. Dr. Henry has developed the finest Prayer Seminar in our nation and it has expanded to an international scale. He is in constant demand across this country for this one-day seminar. Many people say that God moves in one day in the same manner as He would in a week of revival. The results of the seminar are outstanding. Dr. Henry is a very capable teacher, with the gift of preaching and teaching. Your people will be moved to a deeper commitment to Christ and their prayer lives. Just reading the Prayer Seminar Workbook brought a blessing to my life. In addition, Dr. Henry is one of the most interesting speakers I have ever heard. I know you will thank me for this recommendation when you experience the seminar.

Dr. Ben D. Rogers, President
Ben Rogers Evangelistic Association
Jacksonville FL

Dear Dr. Henry:

Having just concluded your prayer seminar here at Goodfellow Air Force Base, we cannot thank you and God enough for the work God has done through you. It was a unanimous consensus that this was by far the best spiritual growth services we have had in memory.

One chaplain who attended the prayer seminar, a seventeen-year service member, stated that he has never been part of a special series of services or workshops for spiritual growth that was better than the one you led us this past month.

Dr. Henry, your prayer seminar ministry is perfectly suited for the military community. Its scope touches the need of Christians from all religious backgrounds. Your presentation is done with a sensitivity and conviction that does not offend the spiritual sensitivities of such a diverse group as a military chapel community, yet touches all involved with the challenge to walk closer to God.

Your prayer seminar has infused spiritual life and excitement into our chapel program. People now have an interest to pray, learn about prayer and walk closer to God. The seminar not only challenged nominal Christians to take seriously their relationship to God but also your seminar opened the eyes of mature Christians who thought there wasn't much more they could know about prayer.

To the person, every participant of your seminar stated that they were touched by God through your ministry and that their prayer life took a definite turn for the better.

We can only say thank you and thank God for your gracious ministry.

Victor J. Toney
Chaplain, Captain, USAF
Protestant Chaplain

Dear Dr. Henry:

The prayer seminar you presented at Goodfellow AFB was absolutely outstanding! It was the highlight of this past chapel year. People are still talking about the favorable impact the Holy Spirit made upon their lives through your ministry.

Your seminar was perfect for the military community. Each night we had every major denomination in attendance. Your appeal is clearly across the board to all Christians.

I've been a military member and chaplain for 18 1/2 years. Never have I had such a life-changing impact on spiritual life of a chapel. I thought I had organized, systematic, daily prayer life. Little did I know all the room

I had for improvement. It has been a month since the seminar and I know of a dozen people who are following what we learned in the seminar. My wife and I are included in the dozen. As a direct result of this seminar, we started a weekly prayer meeting.

Your seminar brought new spiritual life into our Chapel. I highly recommend your seminar to any church or chapel.

Charles Chris Seidlitz
Chaplain, Lt. Col, USAF
Center Chaplain

Dear friend:

I would like to encourage you in every way possible to have a prayer seminar with Dr. Henry.

Dr. Henry's personality is such that he ministers to all ages of people. He brings a wealth of information and experience about the topic of prayer. Combine that with his burden for praying people and you have one of the best and most practical seminars ever presented.

I had the privilege of attending the seminar at our annual staff retreat in May. The seminar brought a fresh awakening to our Missionary Tech Team staff and to me about the importance of intercessory prayer. It was a real treat to be with Dr. Henry for a few days. In all our correspondence prior to the retreat, he was most enjoyable to work with.

In my opinion, this is one seminar that is a must.

Randy W. Harris
Special Ministries
Missionary Tech Team
25 FRJ Drive
Longview TX 75602

Dear Brother Henry:

Your ministry of conducting prayer seminars has been a blessing to those Conservative Baptist churches that have been host to them. The men of our state look forward to your ministry October 24-26, 1985.

I urge others to consider this much much-needed emphasis on prayer.

Your practical and forceful presentation on the subject is most effective. In a time when "programs" get most of the attention in our churches, I appreciate your call to prayer, reminding us that "the fervent prayer of a righteous man availeth much." Many will profit from these meetings.

Dr. Samuel B. Scales
General Director
Conservative Baptist Association of Pennsylvania

For scheduling information and additional information about the seminar (including a sample packet the *Prayer Seminar Workbook*, letters of reference, and a planning guide), write or call:

J. Gordon Henry Ministries
1127 Lakeview Drive
Lynchburg VA 24502-2807
(434) 239-8837
e-mail: jghm84.@aol.com
web address: www.jgordonhenryministries.org

RESOURCES
AVAILABLE

From his prison cell in Rome, Paul wrote to Timothy, his young comrade, in what was his last epistle. As he closed his letter (**2 Timothy 4:9-18**), he explained his situation and urged Timothy to be diligent to come quickly (**v 9**). He asked him to bring Mark (**v 11**), his coat, and his books (**v 13**).

In the early nineties, the Lord impressed upon me the importance of reducing key truths & insights He was teaching me to writing to help His children in their daily walk with Him.

The print and tape ministry provides an opportunity for individuals to study on their own or in small groups—either as review or to further their knowledge and understanding of the essentials of the Christian faith: Bible study, prayer, witnessing, stewardship, and walking in the Spirit as a lifestyle. I have generally used a twelve-study format that lends itself to systematic study for either an individual or a small group. Each year study groups (Sunday school classes, Bible study groups) have used the books as guides for study.

From the beginning, our policy has been not to sell materials, but to depend upon contributions. Most people make contributions, but there are some who either do not, or cannot, make a contribution. This policy has worked and has given us an opportunity to share with many folks.

In order to provide the materials, we need help. Use the response envelope for your contribution (cash or check). Make checks payable to J. Gordon Henry Ministries.

Books:
1. **A Christian's Necessary Food.** Twelve in-depth studies on how to study the Bible profitably. ($8)
2. **Adoration: Prayer as Worship.** Twelve in-depth studies on various aspects of praise and worship in prayer. ($8).
3. **The Enabler.** Thorough study on the Holy Spirit, including how to be Spirit-filled. ($8)

4. **Hey! I'm Saved!** Designed to help a new believer to get started right, the content deals with ten key areas. Why not get one for each Christian in your family? ($3)

5. **Intercession: Prayer as Work.** Twelve in-depth studies on how to engage in intercession as a prayer warrior. ($8)

6. **The Model Prayer.** An in-depth study of the pattern provided by Jesus, Himself, on how to pray. A must for the serious student of prayer. ($8)

7. **Notes from My Bible 2nd Edition.** 1,000 pithy sayings on the Christian life, favorite poems, tributes to Dad Henry and Mom Troutman. ($8)

8. **Spiritual Warfare**. Provides biblical information on our enemy, the nature of the warfare, and God's provision for our protection and victory. ($8)

9. **Upper Room Discourse.** Fifteen studies to help a believer master **John 13-14-15-16-17**, a key section of Scripture in which Jesus' gives final instructions to His disciples just hours before His crucifixion. Excellent to help in understanding the place of prayer and the Holy Spirit in one's life. ($8)

10. **Prayer Seminar Workbook.** The basic teaching tool for the prayer seminar ministry. ($5).

11. **Prayer Seminar Workbook.** An expanded edition (79 pages) that includes content beyond what is taught in a prayer seminar. Both the prayer seminar on cassette and video are correlated to the expanded workbook ($6).

Tapes:

1. **Prayer Seminar Album.** The entire prayer seminar featuring eight hours of teaching correlated to guide a study of the Prayer Seminar Workbook (79 pages). One Prayer Seminar Workbook (79 pages) included. ($16)

2. **Prayer Seminar on DVD.** The entire prayer seminar featuring twelve thirty-minute segments correlated to guide a study of the Prayer Seminar Workbook. Two workbooks (30 pages) included. ($20)

3. **Spirit-filled tape.** Two hours instructing on Bible teachings dealing with Holy Spirit in OT and NT including what Jesus taught and the coming to "all flesh" in the book of Acts. Vital